More Literature Circles

More Literature Circles

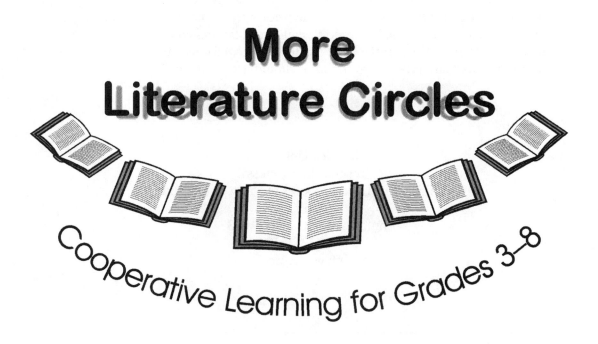

Cooperative Learning for Grades 3–8

Mimi Neamen
Mary Strong

2001
Libraries Unlimited
(Teacher Ideas Press)
A Division of Greenwood Publishing Group, Inc.
Englewood, Colorado

Libraries Unlimited
(Teacher Ideas Press)
A Division of Greenwood Publishing Group, Inc.
P.O. Box 6633
Englewood, CO 80155-6633
1-800-237-6124
www.lu.com

Library of Congress Cataloging-in-Publication Data

Neamen, Mimi.
    More literature circles : cooperative learning for grades 3-8 / Mimi Neamen, Mary Strong.
        p. cm.
    Companion volume to: Literature circles. 1992.
    Includes bibliographical references and index.
    ISBN 1-56308-895-9 (softbound)
    1. Literature--Study and teaching (Elementary)--United States. 2. Group work in education. 3. Children--Books and reading. I. Strong, Mary, 1940- II. Neamen, Mimi. Literature circles. III. Title.

LB1575.5.U5 .N435 2001
372.64'044'0973--dc21   2001038298

Contents

Acknowledgments

We thank our husbands and our children for their patience and support as we worked on this book.

We believe in the inquisitiveness of young minds. We wrote this book for young people, and they are responsible for the direction it has taken.

Introduction

More Literature Circles: Cooperative Learning for Grades 3–8 is for public and private schoolteachers of intermediate-grade students. Although much of the material in the book is written for teachers, there are many reproducible pages for students. The material can be adapted to any teaching style, but it may also be used in the format provided. Teachers may use the books in the first volume in conjunction with the books discussed here. You will find a list of those titles and their conceptual designations in the Appendix.

In this book, a *literature circle* is a group of students reading the same novel, and *cooperative learning* refers to a group working together on the novel to accomplish a common goal or product.

Our purpose is to address the nationwide educational focus on literacy. The program benefits not only the group but also each individual student; it increases the amount of reading students do, provides opportunities for inquiry and critical thinking, and teaches students how to work cooperatively.

Our program is based on our beliefs, assumptions, and observations of how kids learn. We know, because of current research and through experience, that certain elements must be in place in a classroom for students to reach their highest potential. There should be a safe environment in which students interact. Students should be encouraged to bring past experiences to life within current academic situations. Knowledge should be built so that students may apply and analyze it. Finally, students should evaluate what they know to recognize what they still have to learn. Both the interaction with the literature and with other students in the classroom help to make the learning relevant. The combination of literature circles and cooperative learning provides opportunities for decision making, which in turn builds a natural relationship between content and process.

Moreover, submerging students in literature using the literature circle–cooperative learning format creates a community of learners who are finding a way to reach a common goal. The natural engagement in dialogue about their reading nurtures affective and social learning and helps them grasp specific knowledge. Cooperative learning is a support system upon which students build their understanding of a particular concept or idea. In the literature circles, all group members meet on an equal basis, regardless of reading ability, to contribute to a final project that is realized through the combined strengths of all members. The evaluation system ensures that each student is graded not only on group participation and meeting deadlines but also on the quality and appropriateness of his or her contributions.

More Literature Circles begins with a chapter titled "How to Teach with Literature Circles." This chapter consists of explanations of how to implement novel projects and how to use reproducible pages. The second chapter consists of five picture books with related projects. Five picture books, one representing each concept, are included in the picture book chapter. The picture books can be used as a stand-alone unit, or they may be used as a "practice" for the novel projects. The last chapter is divided into five conceptual groupings containing forty novels. Although we have placed each of the forty titles in a particular conceptual grouping, we realize that each title may fit into more than one of the groups. The first novel listed in each grouping is a short one. It can be used in conjunction with the other novels, or it may be used as a whole class "practice" book. Also, to augment the understanding of the concept, we have included a list of "Suggested Read Alouds" with each group. Please use the Read Alouds at your discretion.

So that students might explore an idea rather than discrete knowledge, we chose to organize our sections around concepts. The essence of each concept is focused through an Essential Question. Students read different novels; however, the direction of the thinking that creates the project(s) is similar because of the Essential Question. It is our hope that students will be able to answer the Essential Question resulting from synthesis of evidence from their novel and the novels of others in the conceptual group. The understanding the students demonstrate concerning the Essential Question will vary according to their age and maturity. Certainly, students will benefit from completing their novel and the prescribed projects, but they will find greater benefit from compiling knowledge learned from the presentations of all novel projects to answer the Essential Question. Discussion of the Essential Question following a Read Aloud will help students to practice conceptual rather than discrete thinking.

The literature circles may be interspersed with other activities throughout the year, or they may be used as the entire literature focus of the year. We hope that *More Literature Circles: Cooperative Learning for Grades 3–8* will be useful to all teachers who believe both in the magic and the educational value of reading and in the "joy of story."

Chapter 1

How to Teach with Literature Circles

📖 HOW TO USE THE NOVEL PROJECTS

The following projects use cooperative learning as a base for working with and learning about a novel. The cooperative aspect is stressed in all projects as the students work together to complete assignments using their chosen novel.

The projects are merely suggestions, not dictums. We share the strategies and procedures that have worked well for us. Feel free to make changes according to your classroom population. Throughout this section, we give reasons for doing things in certain ways. In every way, we seek to communicate to the students that we value time spent reading, that ownership of work to come lies with the students, that we will provide opportunities for group decision making and goal setting, that we trust their ability to make good decisions, and that there is a reason to read the novel.

The flexible nature of this book accommodates and promotes a wide range of learning styles, and the novel projects contain activities that address the multiple intelligences, Bloom's Taxonomy, social skill objectives, knowledge objectives, cognitive objectives, and personal involvement. Although we had preconceived notions of what the outcomes of each project would be as we designed them, experience has taught us that many interpretations are possible. Because two broad objectives of cooperative learning in literature circles are to promote problem finding as well as problem solving and to create questions as well as answers, this phenomenon of varying interpretations is one of the beauties of the learning that occurs.

Finally, although we do use and will continue to use these projects in contained classrooms, we feel that cross-grade-level use of the materials is most beneficial to students. The older students set a good example for the younger ones; they demonstrate how responsible they are due to their older age. The younger students emulate the learning behaviors of the older students.

Choosing a Novel

Research supports the fact that choice is essential in creating an environment in which students want to learn. We suggest that groups be formed not by arbitrary or heterogeneous groupings that the teacher formulates but by student choice. We believe choice allows students to exert ownership, and ownership ensures that students will take the best path for their own learning. The reading level of a book is not a main consideration when forming groups; students will readily read a novel if they have chosen it. The novels in this book are arranged, as previously stated, according to concepts.

The following method of selection is suggested because it gives each student a choice.

1. The teacher selects the novels from which the students may choose. There should be multiple copies of each book available because each group should consist of more than one student.

2. The teacher gives a short "book talk" on each title so the students have a basis for selection.

3. Students draw numbers to be used in the selection process.

4. The teacher lists each novel on the board with approximately five slots for students' names under each novel. Be sure to have at least five more slots than you have students; this assures that the student who has drawn the last number also has a choice.

5. The student who draws number 1 begins the selection process. As students choose, write their names under the appropriate novel title. When a particular novel group is filled, students must choose from the other available titles. Complete the selection process with all students.

For a class of twenty-five students, you might choose the following novels from one conceptual grouping and set up your chalkboard in the following manner:

House on Mango Street	*Walk Two Moons*	*Apprenticeship....*
1. _____	1. _____	1. _____
2. _____	2. _____	2. _____
3. _____	3. _____	3. _____
4. _____	4. _____	4. _____
5. _____	5. _____	5. _____

Diary Young Girl	*Lyddie*	*Devil's Arithmetic*
1. _____	1. _____	1. _____
2. _____	2. _____	2. _____
3. _____	3. _____	3. _____
4. _____	4. _____	4. _____
5. _____	5. _____	5. _____

The thirty slots allow for five more slots than there are students. This is important because the student who draws number 25 needs to have a choice of novels.

Beginning Group Work

1. Ask students to sit with their groups.

2. Pass out the novels.

3. Give each group the novel folder (to be kept at all times in the classroom). The folder contains the following items:

   Group Worksheet
   Individual Book Checklist
   Group Novel Checklist
   Daily Checklist
   Group Projects

4. Appoint a facilitator and a checker for each group for the first day.

5. Have each student fill out the Individual Book Checklist.

6. Have each group determine how many pages (or chapters) should be read each day to complete the book in the time allotted (determined by the teacher). We have found that ten schooldays are ample time.

7. The checker fills out the Group Novel Checklist and the Daily Checklist.

8. The facilitator reads aloud the Group Worksheet. This explains the functions of the group and the duties of both the facilitator and the checker. These duties will rotate daily, thus ensuring that each student plays a leadership role in the group.

9. The facilitator reads aloud the Group Projects while students follow on their own copies. Any questions concerning projects should be discussed at this time.

10. The facilitator initiates a discussion concerning the Essential Question. The group members contribute ideas concerning their interpretations of the Question.

11. The group decides whether class time will be spent reading, working on projects, or doing a combination of both. The reading can be accomplished in any way the students choose.

Working with Group Projects

Vocabulary: You may choose whether to use the vocabulary lists given at the beginning of each novel project. If you use them, ask students to discuss the words as they find them in the text. They should try to determine the meaning in context, and the dictionary should only be used as a last resort. Another way to work with vocabulary is to have students generate their own lists.

Group Projects: The projects are self-explanatory. Students may complete the projects in the manner that best suits their group. Some groups do all the projects together. Some groups choose to divide the work among the members. We believe students will make the best choice for themselves and their group. It is important that students are able to make these choices, and it is important that they take the responsibility for the choices they have made.

Presenting the Work

Presentation day(s) is the culmination of the time spent on the projects. The time allotted for this varies with the intricacies of and time needed for the presentations. It is important not to rush any group; they have worked long and hard, and they need to know that their work is valued.

Gather the entire class and determine the order for the presentations. Caution each group to have their projects ready and assembled, and tell them that any special equipment needs to be on hand.

Evaluating the Groups

Performance-based assessment is often difficult to evaluate. We use a two-part system that we have found to be successful, and our students and their parents consider it fair and valuable. Students fill out the Group Evaluation Form twice during the project—once at the halfway point and once at the end. After students have filled out the forms, they discuss the results with the teacher and the other group members. Each student tells what grade he or she assigned to each of the group members and, most important, why that grade was assigned. Students often perceive their own contributions differently from how others perceive them. There is always a marked difference in the quality of group interaction and sharing the day after the midpoint evaluation.

Answering the Essential Question

Students may answer the Essential Question either orally in a discussion format or in a written paper. In fact, a discussion might precede the writing. We believe that answering the Essential Question helps students to practice and hone their critical and creative thinking skills. We believe that metacognition is the ultimate goal of learning; working with Essential Questions is one of the best ways that we have found to attain this goal.

HOW TO USE STUDENT REPRODUCIBLE PAGES

The following items should be kept in each group's folder:

Individual Book Checklist (one for each group member): The purpose for this sheet is two-fold: the teacher has a list of each student's book and book number, and the student knows by looking at the sheet how many pages must be read each day. Each student should fill out this sheet with name, book title, book number, and with the number of pages to be read each day. The group's first cooperative task is to decide how to divide the reading.

Group Novel Checklist (one copy): The first day's checker completes this master list of group members and their book numbers.

Daily Checklist (one copy): The checker completes this evaluation of each group member's daily performance at the end of the day. The evaluation criteria are listed on the sheet. This sheet is a means by which students can see how they need to improve their work in the group. The teacher can also see, at as quick glance, how the various group members perceive each other's contribution to the project. This is a valuable aid to the final evaluation process.

Group Worksheet (one copy): This sheet is read aloud to the group by the first day's facilitator to explain how the group functions and to define the roles of both checker and facilitator. Members of the group may want to refer to this sheet from time to time to clarify roles or responsibilities.

The following item is a reproducible and is not included in group folders.

Group Evaluation Form: One copy of this reproducible is given to each student at both the midproject evaluation and at the final evaluation. The teacher asks each student to fill out the evaluation form honestly and conscientiously. Tell students not to merely rely on their memories but also to look at the Daily Checklist for specific information. It is important that students give reasons for their grades. After Group Evaluation Forms have been completed, meet with each group and discuss the grades with the group. Students should reach a consensus and assign a grade for each member of their group.

INDIVIDUAL BOOK CHECKLIST

Name: _____

Title of Book: _____

Book Number: _____

Number of Pages to Be Read Each Day: _____

GROUP NOVEL CHECKLIST

Title of Book: _____

Names of Group Members:

1.   _____

Book # _____

2.   _____

Book # _____

3.   _____

Book # _____

4.   _____

Book # _____

5.   _____

Book # _____

DAILY CHECKLIST

Book Title: _____

	Date									
Name										
1.										
2.										
3.										
4.										
5.										
Checker's Initials										

Instructions for Grading

1. If the group member has read the assigned number of pages or chapters for the previous day, place a plus (+) in the upper right-hand corner of the appropriate box. If the group member has not completed the assigned reading, place a minus (–) sign in the upper right-hand corner of the appropriate box. Do this at the beginning of each work session.

2. Grade daily group participation in the following manner:

    3 = Good participation
    2 = Medium participation
    1 = Little participation
    0 = No participation

Place the assigned number in the appropriate box at the end of the group work session.

GROUP WORKSHEET

You will read your book individually. How you choose to read is up to you. You may choose to do all reading at home, either silently or with a parent or sibling. You may choose to read in class, either silently or aloud. You also may choose to do a combination of both.

All the work on the group projects will be done together. When discussing how the projects will be completed, you should follow three rules of good group discussion:

1.   Give everyone a fair turn.

2.   Give reasons for ideas

3.   Give different ideas.

Each group will have a facilitator and a checker to ensure that the criteria for good group discussion are met. The roles of facilitator and checker will rotate on a daily basis. Each group member will probably fulfill each role at least three times during the span of the project.

Facilitator: The facilitator sees to it that everyone in the group has an equal amount of time to talk and to listen. The facilitator is also responsible for seeking answers to questions within the group. If the group is unable to answer a question, only the facilitator is permitted to ask the teacher or the librarian for help.

Checker: The checker fills in the Daily Checklist appropriately each day.

GROUP EVALUATION FORM

In the space provided below, list each member of your group. Evaluate each person according to the following criteria (use the Daily Checklists to help you in your evaluation). Give reasons in the space below each name.

1. Equal or extra share of work

2. Consistently a good group member

3. Dependable

4. Reading always completed on time

5. Contributed ideas to the group

6. Work done neatly and with pride

Give each person a grade (A, B, C, D, or F) and tell *why* you think each person deserves that grade. Be honest.

1. Name: _____ Grade: _____

2. Name: _____ Grade: _____

3. Name: _____ Grade: _____

4. Name: _____ Grade: _____

5. Your Name: _____ Grade: _____

Chapter 2

Literature Circles with Picture Books

We have included a section on picture books for three reasons. First, it seems to be easier for students to learn the process of literature circles and cooperative learning using the smaller-scaled picture books and their accompanying projects. Second, using the picture books will allow time for the teacher and the students to practice using an Essential Question to focus the learning on the concept. Third, we love the way picture books tell stories. Many older students think that picture books are for "babies"; this is definitely not so. The picture books we have chosen contain mature and compelling messages for learners of all ages.

IMAGINATION

Greenfield, Eloise (1975). *Me and Neesie*. New York: HarperCollins.

DISCOVERY

Kroll, Virginia (1992). *Masai and I*. New York: Four Winds Press.

JUSTICE AND FREEDOM

Turner, Ann (1987). *Nettie's Trip South*. New York: Scholastic.

EMPATHY

Tsuchiya, Yukio (1988). *Faithful Elephants: A True Story of Animals, People and War*. Boston: Houghton Mifflin.

COURAGE AND SURVIVAL

Siebert, Diane (1991). *Sierra*. New York: HarperCollins.

Me and Neesie

Eloise Greenfield

IMAGINATION

Essential Question: When conventional boundaries of story are removed, how does the unlimited perspective of the author encourage the unlimited perspective of the reader?

Creating an Image of an Imaginary Friend

Neesie is Janell's best friend; however, no one but Janell can see her. Mama, Daddy, and Aunt Bea don't believe that Neesie is real. What do you think Neesie looks like? Does she look like Janell, or does she look different than Janell? Create a likeness of Neesie. A few suggestions include a life-sized cutout or model or a hand puppet.

Having Your Own Imaginary Friend

In what ways would having an imaginary friend be helpful to you? Make a list of some situations in which your imaginary friend would give you confidence or enjoyment. Draw from your list to write a diary entry for one day. What have you and your imaginary friend done on this day? Begin your entry with, "Dear Diary, today _____ and I…." The next entry will describe the day when your imaginary friend leaves. For example, Neesie "leaves" when Janell begins school. When would your imaginary friend leave? Why would she or he leave at that particular time?

Mapping Janell's and Neesie's Actions

In the book, Janell and Nessie are together most of the time. Sometimes Janell is the leader in activities or play; sometimes Neesie is the leader. Make two interconnected time lines that map Jannel and Neesie's interactions. When does Janell lead? When does Neesie lead? How will your time line show the change of leadership?

Masai and I

Virginia Kroll

DISCOVERY

Essential Question: How do discoveries make characters better people, the world a better place, or both?

Mirroring Life Situations

In the book, the illustrations and the text alternately tell the stories of a young, big-city girl and her Masai counterpart who lives in East Africa. Think about your ancestry. Create a picture book in which your current life is mirrored by an ancestor who lives in another country. How would your lives be the same? How would they be different? Include cover, title page, end-papers, text, and illustrations in your picture book.

Interviewing an Older Person

Choose an older person who is familiar with your ancestry. Interview him or her to find out more about what life was like for your ancestors. Where did they live? Did they stay there, or did they move? What were their occupations? What was their education like? What kind of music did they listen to? Are there some stories the older person can tell about your ancestor(s)? Give a brief history of the ancestor, and tell one of the stories to the class. Bring in photos or other arti-facts if possible.

Building a Two-Sided Model

Either choose a scene from the book or an incident from the life of one of your ancestors and create a two-sided model that compares and contrasts the two versions. The model should be three-dimensional.

Nettie's Trip South

Ann Turner

JUSTICE AND FREEDOM

Essential Question: How are our freedoms affected by the constraints of justice?

Creating the Mood Through Art

The illustrations in the book, although not colorful, portray the mood of the story dramatically. Ronald Himmler uses black-and-white shading to intensify the emotions that the story elicits. How do other illustrators use color or the lack of color to set the emotional tone of a story? Go to the library and look at several picture books. Which illustrations stand out for you? Bring at least five examples of art in picture books that you think are effective. Show the illustrations to the class and explain why you think they are so exceptional.

Investigating Slavery in the South

Research slavery in the pre–Civil War South. Tell of your findings in a letter to Addie. Begin by saying, "Dear Addie, after my visit to the South with Brother Lockwood and Sister Julia, I needed to know more about slavery. I found out that…."

Slipping into Another Skin

Ann Turner says, "If we slipped into a black skin like a tight coat, everything would change." If you slipped into a skin other than your own, how would things change? What could you do? What couldn't you do? Present your ideas in written or visual form.

Faithful Elephants:
A True Story of Animals, People and War

Yukio Tsuchiya

EMPATHY

Essential Question: What role does empathy play in the relationship between the reader and the writing?

Portraying the Mood of the Story Through Illustrations

Illustrator Ted Lewin uses dark and light and bright and dull colors to enhance the mood of the story. His colorful paintings symbolize hope and despair. Examine the illustrations carefully. What is happening on the pages where the illustrations are bright and light colored? What is happening on the pages where the illustrations are dull and dark colored? Are there pages that are a mixture of light and dark? What is happening on those pages? Show through color the moods of the story. Create a color palette that, in conjunction with your oral summary, creates the mood and tells the story.

Making an Informed Decision

To "right a wrong," you need to have carefully researched historical facts. Find out the facts surrounding the bombings during World War II preceding Japan's surrender. With this information in mind, what would you have done if you had been the zoo director in Ueno? Present your ideas in the form of a directive to the zoo employees.

Creating a Monument

A tomb on the Ueno Zoo grounds is dedicated to the three elephants and other animals that lived and died at the zoo during the war. This tomb is a monument to these animals. If you could create a monument to something that is important to you, what would that thing be? What would it look like? How would it be inscribed? How would it be decorated? Where would it be located? Build the monument from the materials of your choice.

Sierra

Diane Siebert

📖COURAGE AND SURVIVAL

Essential Question: How do events in a book influence a character's growth?

Writing in the First Person

Diane Siebert writes in the first person. She says, "I am the mountain…." She describes the feelings, the hopes, and the dreams of the mountain. Choose something from nature that you would hope to see preserved. Using the style and perspective of Siebert, write a poem about this natural creation that begins, "I am the _____" and gives reasons for its preservation. Build a strong case for safeguarding the environment of that place.

Creating Cyclical Representations

Throughout the text Siebert speaks of cycles: seasonal, life and death, youth and age, sickness and health, food chain, day and night. Create a visual that represents the cycles described in *Sierra*. You may choose to have all cycles on one page, like a poster, or you may create a book that uses a separate page for each cycle.

Drawing a Parallel

The Sierra Nevada Mountains, as portrayed by Siebert, have courage; they have a strong will to survive. Siebert speaks through the mountain's voice as if the mountain were human. Draw parallels between the Sierra Nevadas and a person. That person might be real or a fictional character. Find characteristics that the character and the mountains have in common. Create a graphic using either words or pictures or a combination of both that illustrates your findings.

Chapter 3
Literature Circles with Novels

📖 IMAGINATION

Essential Question: When conventional boundaries of story are removed, how does the unlimited perspective of the author encourage the unlimited perspective of the reader?

Root, Phyllis (1992). *The Listening Silence*. New York: Scholastic.

Babbitt, Natalie (1975). *Tuck Everlasting*. New York: Farrar, Straus & Giroux.

Conrad, Pam (1990). *Stonewords: A Ghost Story*. New York: HarperCollins Children's Books.

Dahl, Roald (1988). *Matilda*. New York: Viking Kestrel.

Jacques, Brian (1988). *Mossflower*. New York: Avon Books.

Rowling, J. K. (1997). *Harry Potter and the Sorcerer's Stone*. New York: Arthur A. Levine Books.

Winthrop, Elizabeth (1985). *The Castle in the Attic*. New York: Bantam Doubleday Dell.

Suggested Read Alouds

Greenfield, Eloise (1975). *Me and Neesie*. New York: Thomas Y. Crowell.

Henkes, Kevin (1996). *Lily's Purple Plastic Purse*. New York: Greenwillow Books.

Rafe, Martin (1992). *The Rough-Face Girl*. New York: Putnam.

San Souci, Robert (1989). *The Talking Eggs*. New York: Dial Books for Young Readers.

Sendak, Maurice (1963). *Where the Wild Things Are*. New York: Harper & Row.

Steptoe, John (1987). *Mufaro's Beautiful Daughters: An African Tale*. New York: Lothrop, Lee & Shepard.

Van Allsburg, Chris (1979). *The Garden of Abdul Gasazi*. Boston: Houghton Mifflin.

_____ (1981). *Jumanji*. Boston: Houghton Mifflin.

_____ (1985). *The Polar Express*. Boston: Houghton Mifflin.

Wood, Audrey (1987). *Heckedy Peg*. New York: Harcourt Brace Jovanovich.

Yolen, Jane (1989). *Dove Isbeau*. New York: Harcourt Brace Jovanovich.

Yorinks, Arthur (1987). *Hey, Al*. New York: Farrar, Straus & Giroux.

Young, Ed (1989). *Lon Po Po: A Red Riding Hood Story from China*. New York: Philomel.

Zelinsky, Paul O. (1997). *Rapunzel*. New York: Dutton Children's Books.

The Listening Silence

Phyllis Root

Kiri has the gift of healing, but it frightens her. Mali, her guardian who is also a healer, sends her on a vision quest during the winter of her thirteenth year. Despite her fear of becoming a healer, she finds her vision and her new way in the life of the village.

<table>
<tr><td>

Vocabulary

There is a glossary of Native American words in the back of the book.
</td></tr>
</table>

Finding the Vision

Vision quests are a part of many Native American stories and beliefs. Research "seeking a vision," and find out why this was important in the lives of the people. Who went in search of a vision? What happened if the searcher found no vision? After you have done the research, create a short story that shares your findings with the listener/reader. You may choose to illustrate your story.

Being Close to Nature

Most Native American tribes felt close to the Earth and its yield. Byrd Baylor, a Native American from the Southwest, has written several short books about this connection of a people to the Earth; most of her books are beautifully illustrated by Peter Parnall. Read several of her books, such as *Celebration, Everybody Needs a Rock,* and *When Clay Sings.* After finding the rhythm in her poetry, write your own poem about forming a connection with the Earth. Try to illustrate it in the style of Peter Parnall.

Creating a Planetarium

Kiri thinks of the constellations as her friends, her guides. Create a mini planetarium, perhaps in a shoebox with a "peephole" at one end. Make sure your constellations are accurately reconstructed and placed in the "heavens" appropriately.

Dressing Kiri for Winter

The winter during which Kiri found her vision was very cold. How did she dress? Where did she get her clothes? Either create a life-sized replica of Kiri and dress her appropriately, or make paper dolls to represent Kiri. Be sure her dress is in keeping with the descriptions in the story.

Carving Story Beads

Kiri's relationship with her father is kept alive through the story beads that he carved for her when she was a small child. Carve your own story bead(s), and tell the related story.

Designing Your Own Project

If you can think of another project that will clearly demonstrate your understanding of the book, you may substitute it for one of the projects mentioned above. Talk with your teacher about this.

Tuck Everlasting

Natalie Babbitt

The day after Winnie decided to run away from home, she was surprised to find herself being kidnapped by Mae, Jesse, and Miles Tuck. Why was she unsure about how she felt about being taken to the Tuck home, hidden away in the woods? As soon as she met Angus Tuck and learned the Tucks' secret, Winnie was sure she had found true and gentle friends. All she had to fear was if she would be able to guard forever the secret of the magic spring.

Vocabulary	
tangent	p. 3
bovine	p. 3
rueful	p. 9
perversely	p. 27
colander	p. 41
camphor	p. 45
petulance	p. 88
plaintive	p. 104
catholic	p. 120

Illustrating Wheels of Life

Natalie Babbitt refers to Treegap wood as the place where things come together in strange ways. The wood is at the center, like the hub of a wheel that holds things together if left undisturbed. She also describes water traveling from stream to ocean to cloud to stream as a wheel. It forms a circle and continues to turn, never stopping. What other "wheels" in life can you think of? What things happen in a cycle over and over again? Illustrate the "wheels" the author describes in the book and at least three others you have thought about. Show visually what patterns are repeated. Think of what the hub holding the pattern together might be. Use as few words as possible in your illustrations, and place important visual details on the wheel itself.

Conducting a Survey and Tabulating the Results

Angus, Mae, Jesse, and Miles Tuck provide Winnie with insights about what it would be like to live forever. Compile lists of what you think are the good things and bad things surrounding this idea. Then survey other people to find out what they think are positives and negatives about living forever and why. Be sure to remain objective and not let your thoughts enter into your study. Interview your peers, your family members, and other adults. Take notes or ask them to fill out prepared survey sheets. Tabulate the results of your survey, documenting opinions of the people you polled. Also, make a simple graph that shows how many people you surveyed and how many positives and negatives you received.

Creating a Collage of Prisons and Cages

Winnie remembers lines from an old poem: "Stone walls do not a prison make, Nor iron bars a cage." What do you think the author of the poem means by these words? Do you think Winnie imagines there are other things that can make people prisoners? Do you think the Tucks feel imprisoned? What are some other reasons people might feel caged or trapped? Is it possible that handicapped persons could feel caged within their bodies? Can circumstances such as poverty or wealth be prisons? Could ideas be imprisoning? Create an interpretive collage that expresses your ideas. Be as creative and artistic as you can be. When you present your collage, explain what things could also be stone walls and iron bars.

Contrasting Two Settings

The author creates a strong contrast between the Foster environment and the Tuck environment. She describes the Foster way of life as tight and structured. The Tuck way of life is loose and relaxed. Construct the two settings, referring to details from the text. The details will create the contrast between the structured Foster setting and unstructured Tuck setting. You may do two individual constructions, or you may build one model with two sections. When you present your work, describe how the two environments affected Winnie.

Taping an Imaginative Story

Natalie Babbitt takes an imaginative idea and develops it into a creative story that has a message for her readers. There are many picture books that do the same thing. Visit a library and find picture books that you think effectively tell imaginative stories with a message for the reader. Some authors to look for are Robert Munsch, Maurice Sendak, Chris Van Allsburg, and Arthur Yorinks. Choose one book to read on tape complete with sound and visual effects. You may choose to make an audio tape or a videotape. Of course you will want to incorporate drama and expression into your reading. The introduction of your tape needs to include the essence of the author's message and how the author uses imagination to communicate ideas.

Writing a Poem for Two Voices

When Winnie last saw the Tucks, they were leaving with Mae. If she could talk to any one of them again, what might she have said? Write a poem for two voices in which one voice is Winnie's and the other voice belongs to one of the Tucks. The author leaves to your imagination what happened to Winnie and the Tucks between 1881 and 1950 when Angus and Mae find Winnie's grave marker. What do you think a conversation at some time between these years might have been? If you are not familiar with poems for two voices, look at two books by Paul Fleischman.

Fleischman, Paul (1985). *I Am Phoenix*. New York: Harper & Row.

_____ (1988). *Joyful Noise*. New York: Trumpet Club.

Designing Your Own Project

If you can think of a project that will clearly demonstrate your understanding of the text, you may substitute it for one of the projects mentioned above. Talk with your teacher about this.

Stonewords: A Ghost Story

Pam Conrad

The first time Zoe met Zoe Louise, Zoe was four years old, and Zoe Louise was more than one hundred. The lives of the two girls intertwined as Zoe became older and Zoe Louise stayed the same. But time was running out for Zoe Louise, and it was up to Zoe to help her.

Vocabulary	
exoti	p. 1
stonewords	p. 3
banister	p. 7
frankincense	p. 9
translucent	p. 14
pollynoses	p. 14
transparent	p. 36
smudge	p. 57
inexplicably	p. 62
superimposed	p. 70
pulsate	p. 101
brocade	p. 115
foreboding	p. 117

Crossing from Present to Past

The old and new staircases in Grandma and Pop Pop's house are the vehicles for traveling backward and forward in time. Find places in the book where important events take place on the staircases. On a drawing, design, or construction of the staircases, show visually and write about the crossings from present to past that took place there. Arrange the crossings chronologically.

Writing a Time Poem

In our language we have many words and expressions that refer to time and its passage. Examples are in Pam Conrad's poem, "Ghost Time," at the beginning of the book. Brainstorm words, ideas, and expressions having to do with time. From the point of view of one or more of the characters in the book, compose a poem that expresses their feelings and ideas in a meaningful way. When you present your poetry, speak as if you were the character(s). You might choose to dress as a character and carry props to help form the images you wish to convey.

Illustrating Metaphors

Pam Conrad uses metaphors and similes in her writing to create vividly colorful images in the minds of her readers. A metaphor is a comparison of two or more unlike things without the use of "like" or "as." "I was a jack-in-the-box" is a metaphor. A simile is the comparison of two or more unlike things using the words "like" or "as." "Oscar … like a cement garden toad" is a simile. Find at least five metaphors and five similes in the text. Illustrate them and print the words somewhere on the page with your illustration. Publish them in some way to advertise the way metaphors and similes bring written language to life.

Visualizing the Island in the Past and the Present

The island where Zoe and her grandparents live looks very different in the present than it did in the past. The house, garden, playhouse, roads, and cemetery have all changed over the last one hundred years. Construct a visual replica showing what changes have taken place. Your visual needs to have two parts, past and present. Include details taken from the text of the book.

Mapping Time

Zoe Louise says time doesn't make sense. Zoe says, "Imagine that time is no longer the straight line that you're used to, but a curling ribbon turning back on itself over and over. . . ." Map the lives of Zoe and Zoe Louise with curling lines that show how the girls crossed back and forth from past to present. Sometimes their lives were separate; sometimes their lives were intertwined. The shape of your time map, illustrations of important events along the way, and short phrases of explanation will guide your reader in following your map. You may choose to represent the girls' lives with different colors to make their time lines easier to follow.

Rewriting Newspaper Articles

Zoe, Grandma, and Pop Pop read 1870 newspaper articles about the La Barge family and how Zoe Louise died. Now events from the past have been altered. Imagine that you are a newspaper reporter. Write a series of articles for the island's newspaper that tell about the fire, its outcome, and what might have become of Zoe Louise after the fire. Did she ever marry? Did she have children? What did she do with the rest of her life? Publish your articles in an authentic front-page newspaper format.

Designing Your Own Project

If you can think of a project that will clearly demonstrate your understanding of the text, you may substitute it for one of the projects mentioned above. Talk with your teacher about this.

Matilda

Roald Dahl

Matilda is an extraordinary child, a genius. Her parents and her brother, however, are just the opposite. Because they are "half-witted," they treat Matilda miserably. Matilda, in turn, plays wonderful jokes on the family. At school Matilda meets the dreaded and dreadful Trunchbull and the wonderful and loving Miss Honey. Matilda saves Miss Honey from Miss Trunchbull, and, in doing so, saves herself.

Vocabulary	
scabs and bunions	p. 10
instinctively	p. 15
formidable	p. 18
intensified	p. 39
peroxide	p. 64
enraged	p. 67
limerick	p. 78
brogues	p. 83
smock	p. 112
wary	p. 119
newt	p. 137
maggot	p. 161
exalted	p. 171
seraphic	p. 175
phenomenon	p. 179
blithering	p. 217

Contrasting Forms of the Same Language

Roald Dahl is an English author. Some of his language, therefore, is not quite what we are accustomed to in the United States. For example, Mr. and Mrs. Wormwood talk often about the programmes that play on their telly. We would probably talk about the shows we watch on TV. Create a two-column chart; one column is for the British expressions used in *Matilda,* and the other column is for our corresponding American expressions. When deciding how to write the American equivalent, talk with your group members and perhaps with adults as well. Is there more than one way we interpret or say things?

Writing Limericks

Miss Honey asks Matilda to read the following limerick aloud:

> *An epicure dining at Crewe*
> *Found a rather large mouse in his stew.*
> *Cried the waiter, "Don't shout*
> *And wave it about*
> *Or the rest will be wanting one too."*

A limerick is a humorous five-line poem that follows a definite rhyme pattern and has a particular rhythm. Just as music is written in groups of notes called *measures,* poetry is sometimes written in groups of syllables called *feet.* A foot usually contains several unstressed syllables but only one stressed syllable. In limericks each foot contains one or two unstressed syllables followed by one that is stressed. Lines 1, 2, and 5 each have three feet and rhyme with each other. Lines 3 and 4 each have only two feet and rhyme with each other.

Choose five characters from *Matilda* and write a limerick about each one. Because Matilda already composed a limerick about Miss Honey, exclude her. For presentation day, you might want to draw a picture or a caricature of each limerick subject to show to the class as you read the limerick.

Interviewing Matilda

Imagine that it is fifteen to twenty years after the end of the story. Matilda is a guest on your talk show. Why have you invited her to the show? What has she done that makes her newsworthy? How did her life with the Wormwoods and with Miss Honey impact the life she has made for herself? You may either conduct your interview live or videotape it and play the tape for the class. Try to make the interview and the talk-show setting as realistic as possible.

Writing a Poem for Two Voices

If you are not familiar with poems for two voices, look at two books by Paul Fleischman.

Fleischman, Paul (1985). *I Am Phoenix.* New York: Harper & Row.

_____ (1988). *Joyful Noise.* New York: Trumpet Club.

The "normal" Matilda and the "magic" Matilda live in the same body. They sometimes act similarly, and they sometimes act differently. Write a poem for two voices in which the "normal" Matilda is one of the voices, and the "magic" Matilda is the other voice. You may want to talk about many incidents in the story, or you may want to concentrate on a specific incident. Be sure to use the format created by Fleischman. After you have written the poem, be sure to practice it in preparation for presentation day.

Comparing and Contrasting the Film and the Book

Many times movies are made from books. Locate the film and view it. How was it similar to the book? How was it different? You may choose to demonstrate your findings in many different ways. You could create a chart, a series of Venn diagrams, a play that shows the movie scene and then the book scene, a split mural that contrasts the movie and the book, a video that shows clips of the movie and clips from the book.

At the end of your presentation, ask the class to vote on which they think is better, the book or the movie. Tally the votes. Which version did you like better? Why? Be prepared to explain your answer to the class.

Designing Your Own Project

If you can think of another project that will clearly demonstrate your understanding of the book, you may substitute it for one of the projects mentioned above. Talk with your teacher about this.

Mossflower

Brian Jacques

In Mossflower Woods, Kotir, and Salamandastron, the original inhabitants are struggling to hold on to their homes despite the wicked queen's repeated attempts to capture and enslave them. In an action-packed tale about imaginary inhabitants, heroes, and places, Brian Jacques writes about the triumph of good over evil.

Vocabulary	
cowls	p. 44
ponderously	p. 48
abbess	p. 51
chevrons	p. 69
leviathans	p. 69
wraith	p. 70
scapegoat	p. 71
crenellations	p. 95
feral	p. 103
akimbo	p. 104
truculent	p. 179
maelstrom	p. 191
sibilant	p. 191
limpet	p. 237
prise	p. 237
askance	p. 256
impervious	p. 277
obdurate	p. 283
fletch	p. 287
squib	p. 287
hewing	p. 294

Interviewing Brian Jacques

If you were able to interview Brian Jacques in person, what are some questions you would ask him? Good interviewers do their homework before the actual interview. They know a great deal about the celebrities they will talk to. Their questions reflect knowledge of the person's background and work and are deeply inquiring, designed to search out what motivates and moves their subject. You, the interviewer, and another person, the interviewee, need to go to the library, Internet, or any other source available to you to find information about the author of your book. As the interviewer, prepare a list of insightful questions you might want to ask Mr. Jacques.

Share these questions with the person that will play the role of Brian Jacques. As the interviewee, prepare thoughtful, authentic answers to the questions. Act out the prepared interview for your audience on presentation day.

Preparing a Mossflower Meal

The fugitives living in Brockhall have many unusual, but tasty, meals. Prepare a menu for a full course meal consisting of items that might have been served there. Of course you can substitute foods available to you for what might have been served at Brockhall. When you have your menu and list of ingredients completed, prepare enough food so that each group member can have a small taste of everything. Dress as Brockhall characters when you serve your meal.

Reconstructing a Setting

Brian Jacques describes the settings in and around Mossflower in great detail. He makes it possible for the reader to visualize these settings. Each setting elicits an emotion or feeling from the reader. Construct a replica of one of the settings in the book. Include details in this construction that represent the emotion or feeling you experienced when reading about this particular place. Using color and size to emphasize things that are important are ways to convey your thoughts. Your construction and the surrounding areas need to be detailed and have specific references to events in the book that happened in that place.

Writing Acrostic Poetry

There are three major places described in the book: Mossflower Woods, Kotir, and Salamandastron. Could each place represent a major life force? Could Mossflower Woods represent peacefulness and goodness? Maybe Kotir represents war, strife, trouble, and evil. Maybe Salamandastron represents a safe haven and a goal reached after much effort. Throughout the book Gonff creates rhymes and speaks poetically about people and places. Consider what you think is the essence of the three settings and what they represent. Then write an acrostic poem about each setting that expresses your thoughts. Write the name of the place down the left side of a piece of paper. Each letter is on one line.

Follow each letter with a descriptive phrase or word that begins with the first letter on the line and expresses a thought about that place. Your words and phrases should flow into each other without being short and choppy. When your ideas flow from one line to the next, punctuation becomes unimportant. The sum of all the lines reflects your ideas about the meaning of that setting.

Authoring a Wordless Picture Book

Pictures often speak as loudly as words. What mental pictures do you have about what happened in the book? Which pictures are the most vivid and clear? These are probably the most important events in the book, and the story could be told succinctly by showing others these mental pictures in sequence. Imagine that you are a phenomenal illustrator who will tell the story of Mossflower through pictures only. You will author a wordless picture book divided into sections just as *Mossflower* is divided. Your book needs to be long enough to tell the story clearly, but it should not be too long. Publish your book with a cover, endpapers, title page, and contents. Maybe you would like to donate it to your school library after you present it to the group. If you are not familiar with wordless pictures books, look at a book by Chris Van Allsburg.

Van Allsburg, Chris (1984). *The Mysteries of Harris Burdick*. Boston: Houghton Mifflin.

Designing Your Own Project

If you can think of a project that will clearly demonstrate your understanding of the text, you may substitute it for one of the projects mentioned above. Talk with your teacher about this.

Harry Potter and the Sorcerer's Stone

J. K. Rowling

After his parents die, Harry Potter lives with his wretched aunt and uncle and their horrible son, Dudley; Harry's room is a small, dark closet beneath the stairs. At age eleven, though, Harry receives an intriguing invitation to join the student body at Hogwarts School of Witchcraft and Wizardry. Harry accepts the invitation, and the fun and learning begin.

Vocabulary	
craning	p. 1
tyke	p. 2
Muggles	p. 5
parcel	p. 21
specimen	p. 28
gibber	p. 29
gargoyle	p. 54
hag	p. 71
stalagmite	p. 74
stalactite	p. 74
corridor	p. 129
infusion	p. 137

Having Fun with Dudley

The last lines of the book are, "They don't know we're not allowed to use magic at home. I'm going to have a lot of fun with Dudley this summer...." What kinds of things will Harry do to Dudley? How will he repay Dudley for all of the horrible things he did to him before he went off to Hogwarts? Will Harry play mean tricks on Dudley, or will he simply be mischievous?

Creating a Magic Wand

A magic wand has to be a special match for the customer. "The wand chooses the wizard." If you were the customer, what wand would choose you? Why? Look at the wand descriptions in the text as you create your wand. Be prepared to show it to the class on presentation day.

Singing a Wizard's Hat Song

"A rip near the brim opened wide like a mouth—and the hat began to sing: . . ." Imagine that the wizard's hat has other songs besides the "Sorting Hat Song." Make up a song the hat would sing for another reason. Write the words. You may choose to use a tune from a song you know, or you may create your own tune. Your group will have to sing the song on presentation day. Be sure to practice.

Awarding Points

Secretly, divide the rest of the class into four groups. You may keep the names used in the book (Gryffindors, Hufflepuffs, Ravenclaws, and Slytherins), or you may create new names for each of the teams. Design and create a banner for each team. The colors and "logo" should be appropriate for each. Next, you'll need to create a system that defines how you will award points to individuals and to teams. Write down your system. As you go through this literature circle rotation, keep track of the points earned by teams and by individuals. Will teams lose points for rule breaking? Award the points on presentation day. Celebrate the victories of the teams.

Designing a Game

Quidditch is a game that takes place high above the ground. It involves broom-riding players trying to score points with a glass ball. If you could ride a magic broom, if you could become invisible by wearing a special cloak, if you could become a ghost and pass through walls, if . . . , what game would you play? Invent the game, make up the rules, and write a scenario that describes a game being played. Your group members should be some or all of the new game players. Your scenario could be in play form; you might want to create a video of your game.

Researching Magic

There's more to magic than pulling a rabbit out of a hat or sawing a lady in half. Wizards, wizardry, and magic have been part of many cultures. Greek mythology is a good example of magical phenomena as are many of the Native American legends. Arthurian legends also contain wizardry and magic. Choose a myth or legend that contains some kind of magic. Imagine that you were going to write a picture book for young children about this myth or legend. Write an introduction to your book that explains the reason(s) for the magic. On presentation day, give a short overview of the myth or legend; read your introduction to the group.

Designing Your Own Project

If you can think of another project that will clearly demonstrate your understanding of the book, you may substitute it for one of the projects mentioned above. Talk with your teacher about this.

The Castle in the Attic

Elizabeth Winthrop

To soften the news that she is going to return to her home in England, Mrs. Phillips presents William with the best gift of his life. It's an old, real-looking stone and wooden model of a castle with a tiny knight guarding the gates. When the knight comes alive in his hand, William is hooked into Sir Simon's story about a wizard, sorcery, and magic. Suddenly he's off on a fantastic adventure in another place and time.

Vocabulary	
poncho	p. 3
chivalry	p. 9
portcullis	p. 10
drawbridge	p. 10
gatehouse	p. 10
armory	p. 11
buttery	p. 11
scullery	p. 11
allure	p. 12
sacabbard	p. 19
moat	p. 56
brusque	p. 65
stalwartly	p. 69
repertoire	p. 75
legacy	p. 86
trestle	p. 94
squire	p. 97
chain-mail	p. 105
lists	p. 109
rooks	p. 110
gyrations	p. 150
gauged	p. 155
baronial	p. 165

Building a Castle

Construct a model of a castle like the one Mrs. Phillips gives to William. Build and label the rooms and parts using the description of William's castle as a guide. You may use cardboard, paper-towel rolls, sugar cubes, blocks, wood, or any material of your choosing. Make your castle on a sturdy platform so it can be moved. If you need additional information about the design and construction of castles, look at a book by David Macaulay.

Macaulay, David (1977). *Castle*. New York: Trumpet Club.

Designing Castle Flags

The flags waving above castle towers announce to the people that the lords and ladies of the castles are in residence. Family emblems and coats of arms decorate the flags. The objects or designs used in emblems and coats of arms are carefully selected representations of what families and individuals stand for. Design flags for William's castle and Alastor's castle. Your designs need to be representative of the characteristics of the people residing in the castle. Make your designs large enough to be able to use detail, color, and illustration in your interpretation of the characters' traits. You may use fabric, heavy paper, or other materials in your design.

Creating Illuminations

In the Middle Ages, the skins of sheep and goats were prepared for writing or painting upon. This material is called parchment. Its preparation was lengthy and expensive; a little bit had to go a long way. To keep from wasting any space on the parchment when they were printing books by hand, the scribes did not leave any space between the last word of one chapter and the first word of the next. To show where a new chapter began, they made the first letter of the new chapter very large and fancy. These elaborate first letters were often made with gold leaf and painted to set them off from the rest of the letters. These large letters are illuminations. Choose five characters from the book. Write one descriptive phrase about each character. Your phrases need to begin with the first letters of the characters' names. Create illuminations of the first letters of the characters' names (the first letters of the sentences). Make your illuminations elaborate and representative of the traits of the characters. Organize and display your illuminations and phrases in some way. Label your display with the book's title and author.

Constructing a Circular Time Line

The Castle in the Attic has the elements of a "romance" story pattern. In a "romance" there is a hero, an antagonist, a quest or magical journey, a change for the better in one or more of the characters, and a return to the place where the story started. The events of the story make a full circle. Visually show this pattern by placing the events in the story on a circular time line. Your time line may be one-, two-, or three-dimensional. It needs to include events, characters, and settings in the book. On your time line show in some way where in the story a major change takes place in William and represent visually what that change is.

Describing Common Things from a Different Perspective

On page 177, Elizabeth Winthrop describes how William sees the shoes of Mrs. Phillips when she is transformed to her normal size before his size is restored. Imagine that you are as small as one of the lead figures, and everything around you is of normal size. Think of something common with which most people are familiar. Without naming the thing you have in mind, write a description of it from a tiny person's perspective. On presentation day read your description aloud and ask the class to guess what you are describing. If you want to read a book about seeing things through the eyes of small creatures, read a picture book by Chris Van Allsburg.

Van Allsburg, Chris (1988). *Two Bad Ants*. Boston: Houghton Mifflin.

Developing Modern Rules of Chivalry

On page 98 of the book, Sir Simon quotes the rules of chivalry taught to him by his father. Find information about chivalry in medieval times. Are there other rules that Sir Simon doesn't mention? Some medieval rules of conduct are appropriate today, and others are not. Do you think life would be more pleasant if we had modern rules of chivalry? Think of basic rules of conduct that would be appropriate for you today. Ask your peers, your family members, and adults you know what rules they would establish if they could. Decide on a way to state these rules in a pleasing, positive way. Make a poster advertising your new "Rules of Chivalry."

Designing Your Own Project

If you can think of a project that will clearly demonstrate your understanding of the text, you may substitute it for one of the projects mentioned above. Talk with your teacher about this.

📖DISCOVERY

Essential Question: How do discoveries make characters better people, make the world a better place, or both?

Freedman, Russell (1988). *Buffalo Hunt*. New York: Holiday House.

_____ (1983). *Children of the Wild West*. New York: Clarion Books.

_____ (1985). *Cowboys of the Wild West*. New York: Clarion Books.

> **Authors' Note:** This literature circle using the three Russell Freedman titles could be organized in two ways. First choice: students could read only one book and do all or part of the projects. Second choice: students could read two or three of the books and do all or part of the projects. The projects for this literature circle are written generically. They can be applied to any or all three of the nonfiction Russell Freedman books.

Conrad, Pam (1989). *My Daniel*. New York: HarperCollins Children's Books.

DeFelice, Cynthia (1991). *Weasel*. New York: Atheneum.

Hesse, Karen (1996). *The Music of Dolphins*. New York: Scholastic.

O'Dell, Scott (1986). *Streams to the River, River to the Sea*. New York: Fawcett Juniper.

Paulsen, Gary (1990). *Canyons*. New York: Dell.

_____ (1990). *Woodsong*. New York: Bradbury.

Sis, Peter (1998). *Tibet: Through the Red Box*. New York: Farrar, Straus & Giroux.

Suggested Read Alouds

Ackerman, Karen (1988). *The Song and Dance Man*. New York: Alfred A. Knopf.

Base, Graeme (1996). *Animalia*. New York: Abrams.

Curtis, Gavin (1998). *The Bat Boy and His Violin*. New York: Simon & Schuster.

Davis, Andrea (1999). *Duke Ellington: The Piano Prince and His Orchestra*. New York: Hyperion.

Greenfield, Eloise (1988). *Grandpa's Face*. New York: Philomel.

Jukes, Mavis (1985). *Like Jake and Me*. New York: Alfred A. Knopf.

Lester, Julius (1995). *John Henry*. New York: Dial Books for Children.

Martin, Jacqueline Briggs (1999). *Snowflake Bentley*. Boston: Houghton Mifflin.

Schotter, Roni (1997). *Nothing Ever Happens on 90th Street*. New York: Orchard.

Buffalo Hunt

Russell Freedman

Vocabulary	
corral	p. 9
stampede	p. 9
tipis	p. 9
staple	p. 10
tan	p. 12
lodge	p. 20
scalp shirt	p. 20
quiver	p. 23
flank	p. 32
jerky	p. 39
pemmican	p. 39
sinews	p. 41
translucent	p. 42
rutting	p. 45

Children of the Wild West

Russell Freedman

Cowboys of the Wild West

Russell Freedman

Vocabulary	
outfit	p. 9
branded	p. 14
mustered-out	p. 16
stampeding	p. 18
wiry	p. 19
slicker	p. 22
mesquite	p. 22
chaparral	p. 22
jinglebobs	p. 24
rowels	p. 24
bandanna	p. 24
grub	p. 35
aft	p. 50
monotonous	p. 51
tenderfoot	p. 84
legacy	p. 89

Portraying a Culture

The culture of a group of people is defined by its universals of culture. These are geography; food; clothing; shelter; language; education; economy and production; government; art, music, and literature; technology and inventions; customs and traditions; and religion. The combination of text, photographs, and paintings in Russell Freedman books capture many aspects of the cultures of the people he writes about. Choose five universals of the culture represented in your book. Create a photo essay describing these universals. Use your own illustrations or actual photographs you have staged. You may have more that one visual for each universal. The text of your essay should be succinct and well written, and it needs to support your illustrations and photographs. Publish your work with a cover, endpapers, and a title page.

Preparing an Authentic Meal

Russell Freedman tells about the foods that were common a century ago. Refer to the text and prepare an authentic menu for a meal to share with the group. Make a grocery list of what ingredients are needed. Arrange for the equipment and utensils needed to prepare the foods on your menu. Have enough of each course for everyone to have small samples. You will need to substitute some ingredients for those used in the past, but make your foods as authentically as possible. Tell about the foods you serve and talk about how they were prepared one hundred years ago.

Constructing a Typical Shelter

Each group of people constructed unique shelters made of indigenous materials. Russell Freedman describes many of them in great detail. Choose one of the structures described in your book. Make a blueprint or plan for it that names materials to be used and steps in its construction. Build your shelter according to your plan. Place it in appropriate surroundings. Add sufficient detail to make it appear realistic and "lived in."

Finding Patterns

Within a culture certain events occur in patterns that repeat over and over again. One pattern is the seasons: spring, summer, fall, and winter. Russell Freedman refers frequently to the passage of the seasons of the year and of events that are connected with each season. Another pattern might be birth, youth, old age, and death. These repetitive stages in living make life predictable and rhythmic. Find a pattern in your book. What shape could you give to your pattern? A circular shape is often used to represent things happening continuously in much the same way. Create a visual with shape and illustration that represents the pattern you choose.

Composing a Chant or Song and Choreographing a Dance

Much can be learned about a culture through its music. Chants, songs, and dances tell us what life is really like in a specific time and place. Heroes are immortalized, and we learn what personal attributes are admired and valued. Compose a chant or song about the culture and people in your book. Choreograph a dance to accompany it. Set the dance to music. Costumes and props will enhance the performance of your work.

Writing a Monologue and Making a Puppet

Real people are quoted in your book to make factual information more believable. Choose either an actual character or one you imagine may have existed a century ago. Write a monologue (one actor speaking) for your character that tells about one day in the character's life. Write your monologue in first person, as if you are that person. Make a puppet to represent your character. Create authentic clothing and props for your puppet. Ask a friend to help you manage your puppet or read your monologue on presentation day.

Designing Your Own Project

If you can think of a project that will clearly demonstrate your understanding of the text, you may substitute it for one of the projects mentioned above. Talk with your teacher about this.

My Daniel

Pam Conrad

The land that he loves so dearly yields his dream but also kills him. Daniel was only a teenager when he found the dinosaur in the creek bed on the Nebraska farm. Fossil fever was strong during those times, and people even killed for the bones. But it wasn't fossil fever that killed Daniel. Old Julia remembers that time as she tours the Natural History Museum with her grandchildren. She goes back to the family farm in Nebraska and recounts the story of her childhood.

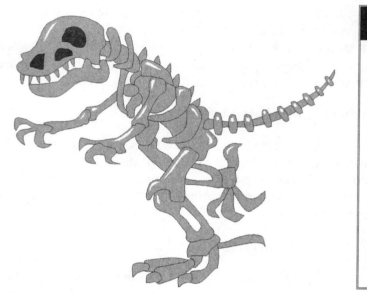

Vocabulary	
hoisted	p. 8
expectant	p. 8
traipsed	p. 9
gnarled	p. 12
crest	p. 14
gruff	p. 24
paleontologist	p. 26
cynical	p. 27
huffing	p. 43
clattered	p. 49
guffawed	p. 75
beacon	p. 111

Building a Soddy

The Creath family, along with many other families who lived on the plains during this time, lived in soddies. What is a soddy? How is a soddy made? After you've found the answers to these questions, construct a model of a soddy. Be sure that the landscape surrounding the soddy is accurate.

Describing Daniel

Julie treasures her memories of Daniel; she describes him in many ways. Go back through the text and write down descriptors of Daniel. What was he like? Describe all aspects of him. After you've gathered all of your information from the book, find a format through which you can share this with the rest of the class. You might want to write an acrostic poem (follow each letter of the name with a descriptive word or phrase),

D _____

A _____

N _____

I _____

E _____

L _____

create an "I Am" poem,

I am (two special characteristics you have)
I wonder (something you're actually curious about)
I hear (an imaginary sound)
I want (an actual desire)
I am (the first line of the poem repeated)
I pretend (something you pretend to do)
I feel (a feeling about something imaginary)
I touch (an imaginary touch)
I worry (something that really bothers you)
I cry (something that makes you very sad)
I am (the first line of the poem repeated)
I understand (something you know is true)
I say (something you believe in)
I dream (something you really dream about)
I try (something you really make an effort about)
I hope (something you actually hope for)
I am (the first line of the poem repeated)

or create some kind of visual representation, or a combination of these things.

Investigating Infant Death

During Daniel's time (mid to late 1800s) and before, many children died in infancy. Daniel and Julie had three siblings who died within hours of being born. Find out why there were so many infant deaths during these early times. What has happened to prevent so much of this from happening now? How can you best show the results of your research? Would a written paper be best? A chart?

Creating a Dinosaur Museum

You have been asked to create the setting for the dinosaur skeletons in a new museum. Choose five dinosaurs (be sure to include the Brontosaurus), and create a habitat for each one of them. You'll need to research the areas in which dinosaurs lived. You may sketch your habitats (use color), or you may build a three-dimensional model. Create the plaques that will explain each of the dinosaurs. Use the plaque description in the book for a guideline.

Hearing the Prairie Night

Jarvis claimed "he could always hear the prairie night" in Julia's ear. What does the prairie night sound like? Who makes the sounds that are heard at night in the prairie? Create an audio tape that plays the sounds of the prairie night. Make a chart or a small book that has pictures and names of the animals that make the sounds.

Designing Your Own Project

If you can think of another project that will clearly demonstrate your understanding of the book, you may substitute it for one of the projects mentioned above. Talk with your teacher about this.

Weasel

Cynthia DeFelice

Nathan and Molly were alone in the cabin when the stranger came. Holding out Mama's locket, he silently and urgently beckoned them to follow him into the night. So begins a journey into fear, hatred, and unsuspected courage. Who is Weasel, and will all he represents win the battle waging inside of Nathan?

Vocabulary	
we-gi-wa	p. 21
buckskin	p. 21
infusions	p. 23
poultices	p. 23
chaff	p. 26
skittery	p. 46
privy	p. 56
addling	p. 59
wrest	p. 60
kin.	p. 72
ruefully	p. 81
aggrieved	p. 94

Writing Notes and Making Gifts

Ezra often left gifts in the wall near the cabin. Later, Molly left notes for Ezra in the same place. Imagine that an exchange between Molly and Ezra takes place beyond what you read in the book. Write authentic notes between Ezra and Molly, and accompany them with authentic, handmade, meaningful gifts. The notes and gifts need to express what you think Molly and Ezra might actually have wanted to say and give to each other.

Comparing the Removal of Two Cultures

The author tells us about the removal of the Shawnees from the Ohio Territory when Congress passed the Removal Act. This is one effort to move a Native American group from one place to another. There are other instances in our history of groups being relocated. Find additional information about the Shawnees, and locate information about the removal of another culture in the United States. How were events surrounding their removal parallel, and how were they different? Show what you have learned in a visual way. You might develop time lines, a Venn diagram, or another vehicle to demonstrate what you have learned. Remember to make your visual large, and use color and space effectively.

Composing Vignettes

A vignette is a snapshot in words of a particular scene or event told from a character's point of view. The same situation could be described differently from another character's point of view. The vignette is written in first person, and the five senses are used to describe the situation in detail. The lines of the piece usually begin with I see..., I hear..., I smell..., I taste..., I touch..., and I feel. . . . Compose three vignettes of scenes or events in *Weasel*. They could be three different situations from one or more characters' points of view, or there might be one situation told from three different points of view. Accompany the reading of your vignettes with visuals and sound effects.

Constructing a Scene from Weasel

Choose a scene from *Weasel* that is vivid in your mind. Construct a model of that scene including details from the text. Place the appropriate characters in the scene. In some way show or tell how you think the characters are mentally reacting to the action in the scene. This might be done with you as a narrator, telling your audience what you think is going through the characters' minds, or you might demonstrate your ideas through a visual addition to your construction.

Creating a Visual of Opposites

Cynthia DeFelice uses analogies in the book to create tension in the characters. For example, conflict raged within Nathan about Weasel. Should he listen to what Pa had taught him and leave Weasel alone, or should he allow his hatred to win and return to kill Weasel? He sees good reasons to support opposite choices. Conflicts in the world today often cause you to examine your own values and morals. Choose two opposites, and think about their implications. Good and evil, justice and injustice, savages and civilized people, war and peace, life and death are some examples. Create a visual such as a collage to represent your thoughts about the concepts you have chosen. Be able to discuss the meaning of your visual.

Coding Personality Traits

The characters in your book demonstrate strong personality traits through their actions and their words. The sum of all their characteristics make them the persons they are. Some characteristics usually considered "good" might work together to create something "bad." Tenacity, for example, usually considered a good quality, shows up in Weasel's abuse of the Shawnee. Create a chart of the major characters and their characteristics, good and bad. Include traits that are obvious, implied, and subtle. Devise a code for the interpretation of your chart. The code needs to demonstrate your ideas about which traits have positive and negative influences on people and events in the book.

Designing Your Own Project

If you can think of a project that will clearly demonstrate your understanding of the text, you may substitute it for one of the projects mentioned above. Talk with your teacher about this.

The Music of Dolphins

Karen Hesse

Mila is rescued from an isolated island off the coast of Florida where she has been raised by dolphins since the age of four. In her new government home, the researchers become her new family. Mila is taught language, music, and what it means to be human; but she longs to return to her warm sea home and her dolphin mother and cousins.

Vocabulary	
flukes	p. 1
molting	p. 2
mangrove	p. 3
cay	p. 3
barnacles.	p. 4
feral	p. 5
recorder	p. 65
ray.	p. 76
orca.	p. 87
pod	p. 130
mullet	p. 179

Exploring Writing Styles

In *The Music of Dolphins,* the style and size of print are representative of what is happening to Mila in the story, with Mila's thoughts appearing in italics. Karen Hesse often uses unconventional writing styles in her books to add impact to the stories she tells. She also often writes in first person so the reader sees unfolding events through the eyes of the main character. You can become familiar with Hesse's writing style by looking at two of her other books.

Hesse, Karen (1992). *Letters from Rifka*. New York: Trumpet Club.

_____ (1997). *Out of the Dust*. New York: Scholastic.

Read enough pages from each book to feel the rhythm of the author's language and to understand the writing style she has chosen to use. Write Chapter 63 of *The Music of Dolphins*. You may experiment with one of the writing styles Karen Hesse used in her books, or you may develop your own style. Either way your narrative needs to be in first person. Publish your chapter in a polished way using illustration to enhance your writing if that appeals to you.

Mapping Mila's Journey

The Coast Guard found Mila in the warm waters between Florida and Cuba. They took her to Miami where she was delivered to the National Institute of Mental Health researchers. From there Mila was moved to a house in Boston near the cold waters of the Charles River. Design and label a map that shows Mila's whereabouts throughout the book. Remember to include her life before the dolphins. Include illustrations and a key. Shade your map in a way that represents the feelings you think Mila was experiencing wherever she was in her journey. When you present your work, explain why you chose the colors on your map.

Constructing a Model of Mila's Home in the Warm Sea

All of the necessities of Mila's life with the dolphins existed on or near the many small cays in the Caribbean Sea between Florida and Cuba. The small islands provided for some of her needs, and the sea provided for others. Refer to descriptions in your book and construct a three-dimensional model of a cay, the surrounding waters, and what Mila needed for survival. You may use clay, cardboard, papier-mâché, or any other appropriate materials in the construction of Mila's environment as you imagine it. Represent details in your model as authentically as possible.

Shaping Changes in Mila

Mila undergoes many changes in the course of the book. Although she is a dolphin girl, she learns quickly and discovers her humanness. Karen Hesse illustrates changes in Mila's character by increasing or decreasing the size of the print and by changing levels of sophistication of the language. You might show changes in Mila by depicting her character visually. Draw a series of shapes or outlines that reflect changes in Mila throughout the story. Within the shapes illustrate or write phrases about events that cause the change the shape represents. Your illustrations and words tell what you think Mila sees, feels, hears, or thinks at different stages in the development of her character. You may use color and shading as well as shape to communicate your ideas.

Composing Dolphin Music and Poetry

Mila composes a little song on her recorder. When she plays it for Shay, Mila feels the music inside. "It says something more than … just the sounds. It is hearing with more than the ears. Like the way it is when I am with the dolphins." Compose a short piece of music that repeats a pattern. Your music needs to reflect a strong feeling you have about something, someone, or someplace that is special to you. Choose the musical instrument on which you will play your music. Experiment with changes in tempo and loudness to express the ideas you are trying to convey. Compose a poem that says in words what you are saying musically. For the performance of your compositions, you may paint or draw a background to stage your presentation. You may be the star performer, or you may invite friends to read and play your poetry and music.

Webbing Mila's Traits

Mila inherited many traits from her dolphin family. The qualities she learned from the dolphins are considered desirable human characteristics. More human traits emerge as Mila spends time with the researchers, Shay, Justin, and Mr. Aradondo. She begins to recognize undesirable human qualities. She questions them and wonders if she will eventually acquire these puzzling characteristics. List the qualities you see in Mila. Kindness, thoughtfulness, loyalty, enthusiasm for life, empathy, and joyfulness are a few. Create a web or map to show Mila's traits and where in the book you see them. Tie in the relationships Mila develops and how other people bring out Mila's qualities. Find a way to code how you perceive her characteristics. Are they good or not good, human or not human? Did she learn them from the dolphins or from her human contacts? Prepare your map or web so it is visually appealing, can be clearly understood, and so that you are able to explain it thoroughly.

Designing Your Own Project

If you can think of a project that will clearly demonstrate your understanding of the text, you may substitute it for one of the projects mentioned above. Talk with your teacher about this.

Streams to the River, River to the Sea

Scott O'Dell

Sacajawea, the young Shoshone girl, twenty-nine-year-old Merriwether Lewis, thirty-three-year-old William Clark, the Newfoundland dog Scannon, and their entourage travel from St. Louis to the Pacific Ocean by way of the Missouri and Columbia Rivers. This is a story of adventure and discovery as Sacajawea is stolen from her own village, won by the Frenchman Charbonneau in a game of chance, and hired to guide the expedition through the high mountains where she was born.

Vocabulary	
drone.	p. 2
roached	p. 6
tunic	p. 15
vermilion	p. 15
resin	p. 17
weir.	p. 27
talisman	p. 27
smirked.	p. 42
keelboat	p. 56
sentinel	p. 77
hordes	p. 134

Drawing the Language

O'Dell depends heavily on similes to enliven his descriptions. One example of this is, "Packs of gray wolves trotted beside them, circling the herds like trusty watchmen." Find at least ten similes and illustrate them. Create a book with your similes (don't forget to put them in quotation marks) and the accompanying illustrations. Put your book together with a cover, title page complete with publisher's information, endpapers, and text.

Creating a Field Book

Clark catalogued all of the flora, fauna, and wildlife he found on his trip. Take a short trip around your neighborhood and catalogue the flora and fauna you find. Draw a picture of a plant, for example, and accompany your drawing with text that further explains it. You should have about twenty entries in your field book.

Mapping the Route

Lewis and Clark begin their historic journey in St. Louis and end it at the Pacific Ocean. Draw a map that traces the route they took. You may need to do some research to find the actual route. Be sure to mark places such as Fort Mandan, the Great Falls, and Beaverhead on the map.

Writing a Poem in Sacajawea's Voice

Imagine that you are Sacajawea. Many years have passed since your journey with Lewis and Clark. You would like to leave a legacy for your children and grandchildren that details your feelings about the journey. The poem should be written in first person, and it should be more emotional than purely a recounting of the trip. Find a way to tell the audience, in the first few lines of the poem, that you are Sacajawea without saying so directly. You may illustrate your poem if you like. Be prepared to present the poem orally to the class.

Researching the Newfoundland

What is a Newfoundland? Where would Lewis have gotten the dog? Either show the class a picture of the dog, or bring in a real Newfoundland. Make a poster that tells about the dog.

Designing Your Own Project

If you can think of another project that will clearly demonstrate your understanding of the book, you may substitute it for one of the projects mentioned above. Talk with your teacher about this.

Canyons

Gary Paulsen

Fifteen-year-old Brennan Cole is a runner from El Paso, Texas. He doesn't run for a track team or to stay in shape; he runs "to be with himself." While camping in a mountain canyon, Brennan finds a skull that has been pierced by a bullet. He learns that it is an Apache boy's skull; the boy was executed by soldiers in 1864, Now, more than one hundred years later, the spirit of the Apache boy, Coyote Runs, comes to Brennan. Brennan hears the message Coyote Runs gives, and he takes the skull to the medicine place.

Vocabulary	
gully	p. 18
scowling	p. 35
mesquite	p. 46
hyper	p. 49
condensing	p. 53
swale	p. 58
vaqueros	p. 59
faltering	p. 65
reluctant	p. 68
warble	p. 81
archives	p. 130

Investigating the Quakers

Coyote Runs and Magpie went to a Quaker school to "learn how to be white." Who were the Quakers? What were their beliefs? Were they really in New Mexico in the 1860s? Did they work with Apaches and other Native American Tribes? Are there still Quakers today? Where do they live? What do they do? Have their beliefs changed? Remained the same?

Mapping the Territory

Paulsen accurately describes the region where the story occurs, which includes New Mexico, Texas, and Mexico. Draw a map of this area. Be sure to include places specifically mentioned in the book such as El Paso, White Sands, the Organ Mountains, and Alamogordo. Can you locate Dog Canyon? Trace the route Coyote Runs and the other Apaches took when they went on the horse raid. Did they return the same way they had gone?

Researching Apaches

Apaches still live in this area of New Mexico. How have their lives changed in the last 150 years? You'll need to find out how the Apaches lived in the mid-1800s and how they live now. What kinds of things happened to precipitate these changes? Report your findings in some kind of visual way. You may choose to create a mural, a pictorial and verbal time line, a picture book. Be prepared to present your rendition to the class on presentation day.

Writing **I Am** *Poems*

Using the following format, write two *I Am* poems-one as if you were Brennan (at the end of the story) and one as if you were Coyote Runs.

I am (two special characteristics you have)
I wonder (something you're actually curious about)
I hear (an imaginary sound)
I want (an actual desire)
I am (the first line of the poem repeated)

I pretend (something you pretend to do)
I feel (a feeling about something imaginary)
I touch (an imaginary touch)
I worry (something that really bothers you)
I cry (something that makes you very sad)
I am (the first line of the poem repeated)

I understand (something you know is true)
I say (something you believe in)
I dream (something you really dream about)
I try (something you really make an effort about)
I hope (something you actually hope for)
I am (the first line of the poem repeated)

You'll want to share both an oral and a visual copy of this poem on presentation day.

Designing a Memorial

If Brennan could have designed a memorial to Coyote Runs, how would it have looked? From what would it have been created? Where would it be placed? Would it have words? Create in either two or three dimensions a memorial to Coyote Runs. Explain why and how you have designed and created it in this specific way.

Designing Your Own Project

If you can think of another project that will clearly demonstrate your understanding of the book, you may substitute it for one of the projects mentioned above. Talk with your teacher about this.

Woodsong

Gary Paulsen

Through his vivid language, Paulsen gives a look at a man who thought he knew about nature and the outdoors. Instead, the dogs he trains and races make him realize how little he really knew. In time their lessons help him understand and appreciate the world of nature.

Vocabulary	
paradox	p. 1
gulled	p. 2
trapline	p. 2
gangline	p. 2
preconceived	p. 6
amuck	p. 9
bounty	p. 10
standoffish	p. 11
relative	p. 13
genetic	p. 14
alleviate	p. 22
lobes	p. 26
chagrin	p. 28
ruff	p. 28
popple	p. 31
blown	p. 35
clutch	p. 44
obese	p. 47
smudge	p. 59
pathological	p. 62
hallucinating	p. 96
mandatory	p. 103
stultifying	p. 113

Presenting Information About the Iditarod

Alaska's Iditarod is sometimes called "The Last Great Race." It involves years of planning and preparation by the mushers and their teams. The organization of it is important for safety and efficiency. Find out about the many aspects of the race: the preparation for it, rules and regulations for mushers and dogs, supplying the teams, how the race is observed and reported, historical significance, information about the dogs, and other details. Organize your information and then present it orally and visually with props and visual aids. Be imaginative in the format you choose to share your information.

Building a Model of a Sled

Paulsen says the dogs are "the true athletes of the Iditarod," and a well-equipped sled enables them to maintain their strength. Build a model of a dogsled that might be pulled by a team in the Iditarod. Construct the sled so that you are able to show how the dogs are harnessed to it. Be sure you include in your model replicas of the equipment that a musher would carry in the race, and be able to explain how the items are used. Your representation could be large or small. Maintain as much authenticity as possible.

Mapping the Events of the Race

Gary Paulsen recounts vividly and sometimes humorously events that stand out in his mind during the seventeen-day Iditarod. A map of the race and its checkpoints is located at the beginning of your book. Draw and label a similar map of Alaska and surrounding areas. On your map place one-, two-, or three-dimensional illustrations or figures to show the events on days one through seventeen of Paulsen's race. Try to match details of your illustrations or figures to the details of the author's descriptions of the race.

Expressing Yourself Poetically

The author's way with language creates vivid images in his readers' minds. He also communicates his feelings in his writing. Phrases such as "dancing with winter" give readers a sense of the emotions he experiences in a situation. Think of an experience or an emotion you have had that is brought to mind by something in the book. Write a piece of poetry about it. Or write a poem from a character's point of view about something in the book that elicited strong emotions in you. Accompany your writing with a visual interpretation of the event or feeling.

Creating a Learning and Questioning Collage

Paulsen realizes he does not understand much about nature. "I didn't know what I didn't know." As a result of keeping and running his dogs, he learns many lessons that help him better understand the world around him. As you read, take notes about the lessons the author learns. Quote the author as often as possible. Compose a list of questions you think might have helped Paulsen in his learning when he began his dog experiences. When you have your lessons learned and your quotations and questions, put them all together in a collage. Combine language and visuals in your collage.

Writing and Sending a Letter to Gary Paulsen

Mr. Paulsen's life experiences are reflected in his writing. What personal characteristics do you think contribute to his style of writing? Biographical information about the author may provide insight about the person that wrote *Woodsong*. Factual information about Paulsen may help you learn about the person as well as the writer. Library reference books and sites on the Internet are good resources to help you. Think of comments and reflections you have about his book and questions you might have for him. Write a thoughtful, sincere letter to mail after presentation day. Maybe you want to talk about the way he uses humor to make serious subjects seem "light."

Maybe you would like to tell him what parts of the book you like or dislike and why. Address an envelope to Gary Paulsen in care of the publisher using the address on the back of the book's title page. If you enclose a self-addressed, stamped envelope, your chances of receiving a reply will increase.

Designing Your Own Project

If you can think of a project that will clearly demonstrate your understanding of the text, you may substitute it for one of the projects mentioned above. Talk with your teacher about this.

Tibet: Through the Red Box

Peter Sis

For most of the author's childhood, the red box in his father's study has held mysterious secrets. Now his father calls Peter Sis home for these mysteries to be unveiled. He finds the diary his father kept while lost in Tibet in the mid-1950s. The contents are a blend of truth, dreams, and memory, and the story that emerges is a treat for the imagination.

Vocabulary

The vocabulary section consists of the Tibetan words and terms woven into the text of the book. Because the author tells the meanings of the words in the context of the story, it is unnecessary to define them further.

Weaving a Tapestry of Truth, Dreams, and Memories

Peter Sis discovers that his father's diary weaves together truth, dreams, and memory in its stories. As you read the book, keep a chart of events, people, and places that are mentioned. Using reliable sources of information and your own intuition, determine which of these are factual (truth), which are dreams (imagined), and which are told from memory (may be based on fact but are exaggerated). You must be able to verify that the factual information is indeed the truth. Design and weave a tapestry that depicts the blend of truth, the dreams, and the memories of the events, people, and places in your book. Your viewer needs to be able to distinguish between them. You may make your weaving of fabric, paper, or another material. Use color, shape, and size to help interpret your ideas. Peter Sis offers clues about the significance of color and shape in the Tibetan culture.

Making a Relief Map of the "Roof of the World"

Because Tibet and the Himalaya are the highest places on the Earth, they are known as the "Roof of the World." Make and label a relief map that shows this part of the world and where it is located in Eurasia. Your map needs to encompass China, Nepal, the countries that were Czechoslovakia and the Soviet Union, and other surrounding European and Asian countries. Label the Himalaya, Moscow, Beijing, Lhasa, and the Lhasa Highway. The title page of your book gives you a good idea of the approximate area of your map. Also, find information about the iron curtain that Peter Sis says surrounded his country. Be able to tell what and where it was.

Constructing a Tibetan Scene

A farmer's home, the Potala, the Valley of the Giants, the Blue Lake, and other scenes are described in some detail in your book. Create a scene as Peter Sis describes it; however, use your imagination to add to and embellish the scene. Use materials of your choice to construct a three-dimensional version of how you and the author envision the place. Include numerous details to make it vivid and lifelike.

Creating a Mandala

Peter Sis quotes his father's diary: "We see wheels of life painted everywhere, symbolizing life as it really is." These circular, colorful, detailed wheel illustrations are found throughout the book. The Tibetans call them mandalas. In the book they describe symbolically what is happening in the story. Think about what might happen next if the diary had continued. Create a mandala that describes visually what you think occurs next. Circles and other geometric shapes, vivid colors, symbolism, and painstaking detail are the most important features to keep in mind as you design your mandala. Use the media of your choice in your creation. Fabric, paints, colored pencils, and pastels are some options. Close examination of the illustrations in your book might help you in your work.

Reporting from Two Points of View

The Chinese authorities speak negatively about the Tibetan people and their world. The Chinese say Tibet is part of China and Tibetans are primitive barbarians living in the region of "The Dark Mountain." The author's father views Tibet and its people very differently. His view of Tibet and Tibetans is warm and positive. Imagine that two newspapermen are commissioned to write about the Tibetans and their country. One reporter writes from China's point of view. The other reporter writes about the same thing but from the point of view of the author's father. Obviously the two articles will be vastly different. Publish your articles in a newspaper format with headlines, bylines, and pictures. Use information from your book and from any other source you may find.

Comparing the Tibetan Culture and Your Culture

Cultures all have "universals" in common. We can describe and compare cultures by examining their geographies, foods, clothing, shelters, languages, education, economies and production, governments, art, literature, music, technology and inventions, customs, traditions, and religions. The author's father found many reasons to admire the Tibetan culture. He found the people to be easygoing, fun loving, and devout. Many things about their culture that make them unique are mentioned in the book. As you read, keep a record of as many Tibetan cultural universals as you can find. Then think about the cultural universals of your culture. With these two sets of information, you are able to compare the Tibetan culture to your culture. Create a written or visual chart that shows your comparisons. The format of your chart can be of your choosing.

Designing Your Own Project

If you can think of a project that will clearly demonstrate your understanding of the text, you may substitute it for one of the projects mentioned above. Talk with your teacher about this.

JUSTICE AND FREEDOM

Essential Question: How do the constraints of justice affect our freedoms?

Fleischman, Paul (1998). *Whirligig.* New York: Dell.

Fleischman, Sid (1987). *The Whipping Boy.* New York: Greenwillow Books.

Hesse, Karen (1993). *Letters from Rifka.* New York: Penguin Putnam.

Paulsen, Gary (1993). *Nightjohn.* New York: Delacorte Press.

Speare, Elizabeth George (1976). *The Witch of Blackbird Pond.* New York: Bantam Books.

Taylor, Mildred D. (1977). *Roll of Thunder, Hear My Cry.* New York: Dial Press.

_____ (1987). *The Friendship.* New York: Dial Press.

> **Authors' Note:** In this grouping, Mildred Taylor's short novel, *The Friendship*, is the suggested whole class "practice" book.

Suggested Read Alouds

Hooks, William H. (1996). *Freedom's Fruit.* New York: Random House.

Hopkinson, Deborah (1993). *Sweet Clara and the Freedom Quilt.* New York: Alfred A. Knopf.

Lawrence, Jacob (1993). *The Great Migration.* New York: HarperTrophy.

Say, Allen (1994). *Grandfather's Journey.* Boston: Houghton Mifflin.

Scieszka, Jon (1989). *The True Story of the Three Little Pigs.* New York: Viking.

Thomas, Joyce Carol (1998). *I Have Heard of a Land.* New York: HarperCollins.

Turner, Ann (1987). *Nettie's Trip South.* New York: Scholastic.

Williams, Sherley Anne (1993). *Working Cotton.* New York: Harcourt Brace Jovanovich.

Whirligig

Paul Fleischman

Brent Bishop, a seventeen-year-old high school junior, has a hard time "fitting in." He seems always to be the odd man out. Finally, the family moves to Atlanta, and Brent's father gets a job that will allow Brent to go to a private school. This move and the new school prove to be no better. Brent's schoolmates shun him, one girl particularly. He tries to destroy himself in a car crash, but he kills Lea, an innocent teenage girl, instead. As restitution, Lea's mother asks Brent to memorialize Lea by building four whirligigs, one at each corner of the country.

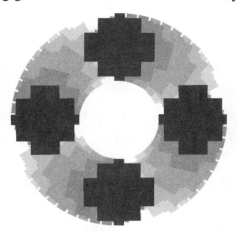

Drawing Brent's Whirligigs

Mrs. Zamora has only one request of Brent—that he make four whirligigs of a girl that looks like Lea, put her name on them, and set them up in the four corners of the United States. She says, "Let people all over the country receive joy from her even though she's gone. You make the smiles that she would have made. It's the only thing you can do for me." Find the descriptions of the four whirligigs in the book. Draw pictures not only of the whirligigs but also of the surrounding environments. You may have to do some research on the specific areas of Washington, California, Florida, and Maine.

Creating a Whirligig

Brent found, in a dingy old bookstore, a book called *Make Your Own Whirligigs and Weathervanes*. Find directions for making a whirligig, either on the Internet or in a book. Using materials similar to the ones Brent used, create a whirligig that represents the spirit of something or someone you would like to memorialize. Make your whirligig and bring it to show the class on presentation day.

Making Your Own Music

After listening to the man play the concertina, Brent bought a harmonica and an instruction book. "He'd try his hand at making his own music." What would you like to do that you've never tried? How would you go about learning? Would you have to buy special equipment? Take lessons? Do research? Create a plan that details, step-by-step, how you would learn something new. If you need to buy equipment, where will you get it, and how much will it cost? How much do lessons cost? Who will teach you? Find out all the pertinent information.

Sending a Wave Rolling Out of Sight—Leaving a Legacy

Miss Gill, Brent's mediator in Chicago, told Brent that "the effects of an act traveled far beyond one's knowledge." Brent knew that she meant harmful acts, but he believed the same could be true of good deeds. Many people have left legacies both to people they knew and to humanity in general. Create a chart on which you will list at least ten famous people and their legacies, at least eight fictional characters and their legacies, and at least three people you know personally and their legacies. Also, think about what your legacy might be.

Tracing Brent's Route

Create an outline map of the United States and trace Brent's route. Be sure to mark his stops. If a particular area is described in the book (such as the saguaro cactus on page 87), illustrate that on the map. This should be more than a normal route on a map. The audience should be able to see some of the sights Brent saw.

Describing Cause and Effect

Fleischman says in the next-to-last paragraph of the book that "The world itself was a whirligig, its myriad parts invisibly linked, the hidden crankshafts and connecting rods carrying motion across the globe and over the centuries." How are events in the world connected? How has what happened in the past influenced the present? Think of how our culture is based upon other cultures. Think about what you've studied in social studies, and make some kind of visual that depicts how one event in history caused another event.

Designing Your Own Project

If you can think of another project that will clearly demonstrate your understanding of the book, you may substitute it for one of the projects mentioned above. Talk with your teacher about this.

The Whipping Boy

Sid Fleischman

Jemmy dreams of running away, back to the streets from which he had been plucked to receive the whippings earned by Prince Brat. Little did Jemmy suspect that Prince Brat has his own ideas about running away. Together they begin an adventure that will change their lives forever.

Vocabulary	
cuff	p. 2
common	p. 2
contrite	p. 4
scragged	p. 8
cleaver	p. 11
chortled	p. 14
rogues	p. 14
heft	p. 18
curs	p. 20
mangy	p. 20
flummox	p. 21
paltry	p. 25
scoffed	p. 27
insolent	p. 27
blanched	p. 28
parley	p. 34
amber	p. 46
derelict	p. 75
manacle	p. 77

Creating a Wordless Picture Book

At the beginning of the book, Jemmy thinks that freedom means getting away from the castle. At the same time, Prince Horace wants to be free of all the constraints in his life. By the end of the book, each boy learns what true freedom really means. The author provides numerous clues to the reader that changes are taking place in the boys' thinking. Certain events were turning points in the boys' lives. Some pivotal moments are when Jemmy refers to Prince Brat as "friend," when Jemmy hears Prince Brat laugh for the first time, when Jemmy loses his taste for ignorance, when Prince Brat realizes how folks in the kingdom really feel about him, and when Jemmy wonders if clothes make a prince. Create a wordless picture book that shows pictorially these and other changes in the two characters. Precede the pictures in your book with well-chosen titles, much as the author titled each of his chapters. These will be the only words in your book. Publish your book with a cover, endpapers, title page, dedication page, and the contents. If you are not familiar with wordless picture books, look at a book by Chris Van Allsburg.

Van Allsburg, Chris (1984). *The Mysteries of Harris Burdick*. Boston: Houghton Mifflin.

Deciding What Makes a Prince and a Commoner

Jemmy wonders, "Was it clothes that made a prince, just as rags made a street boy?" Think about what qualities you think make a prince or a street person (commoner). How do people's actions influence how other people perceive them? Could people that appear ragged and poor really be princely? Could people that appear well dressed and wealthy really be "common?" How important are appearances? What qualities in people really determine if they are princes? What traits do people have that make them commoners? In a visual way, represent your thoughts and ideas about these questions. Show visually what qualities, characteristics, actions, or words contribute to making people who they are. You may choose to use magazine or newspaper pictures and words, or you may create the visuals yourself.

Replicating a Medieval Fair

In medieval times fairs were held in cities or at heavily traveled road intersections. Here could be found goods and entertainment that attracted people of all kinds from nearby castles and villages. Fairs were big events, and a variety of activities enticed travelers and merchants to come to them. Using a variety of sources, including your book, find information about medieval fairs. Construct a model with replicas of what might be found there. In place of labels, make signs to identify the parts of your model. Include the ballad singer and the town crier in addition to booths, sellers, and goods.

Designing Coats of Arms

During the middle ages, coats of arms were designed to symbolize what a person or family was known for. Their characteristics, strengths, livelihoods, dreams, and accomplishments were advertised through these designs. They appeared on banners and shields. Design two coats of arms for Jemmy and two for Prince Brat. The first design represents the character of each boy at the beginning of the book. The second represents the growth and changes in the two characters by the end of the book. Be prepared to explain your ideas represented in your four coats of arms.

Composing Ballads for Two Characters

On page 72 the ballad seller sings a ballad about Hold-Your-Nose Billy. This was a sample of his merchandise. He might also have had ballads to sell about rat-catchers, Cutwater, Ol' Johnny Tosher, Petunia, the king, Prince Brat, or others. Choose two characters from the book and compose ballads that capture the essence of their personalities and how the common folk perceived them. Your compositions need to be rhythmical and catchy. Accompany the performance of your ballads with music.

Creating a Fact or Fiction Game Show

Sid Fleischman tells the reader that the practice of keeping whipping boys is true. Do you believe that? Search out other interesting facts about the Middle Ages that seem stranger than fiction. Mix in some untrue fictitious statements that you make up. Create a *Fact or Fiction Game Show* in which the contestants gain or lose points according to their ability to guess if the clues you give them are fact or fiction. You may choose to model your game after one with which you are familiar or devise a format of your own. Prepare the rules for playing, the rules for scoring, the game board, questions for the contestants, props, and other components of the game to make your show informative and entertaining.

Designing Your Own Project

If you can think of a project that will clearly demonstrate your understanding of the text, you may substitute it for one of the projects mentioned above. Talk with your teacher about this.

Letters from Rifka

Karen Hesse

Freedman, Russell (1980). *Immigrant Kids*. New York: Scholastic.

> **Authors' Note:** This literature circle is about *Letters from Rifka*; however, the Russell Freedman book, *Immigrant Kids*, is used as a reference book for two of the projects. Students may read only the parts of the book mentioned in the project guidelines. Because it is relatively short, however, students may decide to read the entire book.

Rifka, her two brothers, and her parents leave Russia in September 1919. In *Letters from Rifka*, she tells her cousin, Tovah, about the events leading to her arrival at Ellis Island in America. *Immigrant Kids* is a photo essay about immigrant children in New York City: their coming over, their home, their school, their work, and their play.

Vocabulary	
rucksack	p. 3
regiment	p. 4
battalion	p. 8
stench	p. 18
fumigation	p. 19
cossacks	p. 22
typhus	p. 23
ringworm	p. 42
monitor	p. 49
etched	p. 51
mitzvah	p. 54
shirring	p. 69
davening	p. 69
peruke	p. 71
parquet	p. 76
samovar	p. 87

Retracing Rifka's Journey

On a world map that you have made, trace Rifka's journey from Berdichev, Russia, to Ellis Island near New York City. Include all of her stops, the major cities she was in or passed through, and bodies of water she crossed. Add small illustrations or three-dimensional features to indicate the events that took place along the way. At what point in the book do you think Rifka stopped looking backward to her home in Berdichev and started looking forward to her life in America? Show her change of heart and attitude on your map. You might use color, shape, size, illustration, or other techniques to show the change in Rifka.

Logging History on a Time Line

The author's Historical Note talks about what was happening in Russia at the time around World War I. Locate further information about historical events during this time period. Why were Jews being persecuted? What is a *pogrom*? Why did government officials allow Rifka's brothers to be treated as they were? After gathering your information, log events you have researched on a three-dimensional time line. Present in an interesting way what you have learned so that your audience will understand the background of events in your book.

Charting Injustices and Freedoms

Within her letters to Tovah, Rifka speaks of injustices she and other Jews in Russia have to accept as part of their way of life. For example she asks, "Why … a Russian peasant … feels justified in stealing … from a Jew?" Also, Mama tells her to stop sniffling about the missing candlesticks and just get dressed. As you read, keep a list of things in the book that seem unjust to you. When possible, give page numbers and direct quotations as evidence. After you have your completed list, read the Bill of Rights and the amendments to the Constitution of the United States. For each injustice found in your book, find a freedom that these documents ensure and that in our country would prevent persecution like that which Rifka and her family endured. Make a visually creative chart that shows the injustices you found and the freedoms that counterbalance them.

Writing a Letter from Rifka

At the end of the book, Rifka tells Tovah that she will write her a real letter. What do you think this letter will say? Will Rifka write about her life in America? How do Rifka and other children see their lives in their new homes? In *Immigrant Kids* the author writes about what home, school, work, and play were like for immigrant children. Read pages 15 through 67 to get the flavor of what life was really like for children like Rifka. Write a letter from Rifka to Tovah about her life in America. Put yourself in her place and write as if you were she. Think about Rifka's writing voice in the book and try to model your writing voice after hers. Remember that your letter and envelope need to be done in an authentic style.

Making Hats for Characters

Rifka's black velvet hat with the shirring and the light blue lining symbolizes new confidence and hope to her. Choose four characters from the book. Create hats that represent what you think are their strongest features and characteristics. Your hats might be of an actual size that can be worn, or they might be smaller and placed on puppets. Think about what your chosen characters might have to say and what they might think after living in America for a while. Write a short first-person script for each character. When you present your work, you may read the script and wear the hat for all the characters; or you may ask friends to help you portray some of the characters.

Constructing a Model of Ellis Island

Papa says that Ellis Island is a line separating Rifka's future from her past. Russell Freedman says that it was known as "Heartbreak Island" among the immigrants. Read pages 1 through 14 in *Immigrant Kids*. Then go to the library and find additional information about Ellis Island. Construct and label an authentic model of Ellis Island and surrounding areas. Include New York Harbor, the Statue of Liberty, the Hudson River, New York City and lower Manhattan, the pier, the ferryboats, and the buildings where the immigrants went. Practice how you will present your model to the group.

Designing Your Own Project

If you can think of a project that will clearly demonstrate your understanding of the text, you may sbstitute it for one of the projects mentioned above. Talk with your teacher about this.

Nightjohn

Gary Paulsen

Nightjohn, a slave himself, brought reading and writing to other slaves. Even though Master Waller chopped off Nightjohn's toes, it didn't stop him from teaching lessons. Sarny, a young slave girl, tells the story of learning what the letters mean and how to put them together to form words. We learn more than reading and writing from the story, though; we learn the history of a culture.

Creating a Symbolistic Collage

Nightjohn, Sarny, and Mammy each are "governed" by an idea, a thought. This thought is never out of their minds and leads them to accomplish what they do and to act as they do. Create a three-paneled collage. Title each of the panels with the names of the three characters. After you've determined the governing word for each of the three, decide how you will depict this word. What symbolizes this word for you? The rest of the collage should surround and support the governing word. Everything on the panel should radiate from your depiction of the word. Think, as you begin to create the collage, about colors and what they symbolize.

Debating the Pros and Cons of Returning to the Plantation

Nightjohn has been free; he has escaped to the North. Why does he decide to return to the plantation? Create a dialogue that Nightjohn might have had with himself as he decides whether to return or to stay free. What will each "side" of his personality say? What will the arguments be? Use documentation from the text. Two group members should perform this debate on presentation day. How will you stage the debate so that the audience gets the idea that it is the two sides of Nightjohn's own mind that are debating?

Researching the Underground Railroad

Many slaves escaped bondage via the Underground Railroad. What exactly was this? How did it work? Imagine that you run one of the stations on the Railroad. What sign do you set out to let the runaways know that it is safe or unsafe? What happens if slave catchers or some other authorities come to your home while runaway slaves are there? Write a short skit that will demonstrate for the class what it was like to be a part of that system. Perform the skit for the class on presentation day.

Taking a Visual Journey

Using whatever medium you prefer, create a visual journey through the book. You could illustrate a book, create a video, or perform a live play. You will want to choose your scenes carefully; they should connect with each other. You may choose to narrate the journey; you should have appropriate background music. Keep the narration to a minimum, and let the music provide background rather than a focus of the journey. Your focus should be visual.

Predicting the Future

What will Sarny do next year, or in the next five or ten years? Why do you think her life will take this certain direction? Use quotes from the book to support your theory. Write a letter from Sarny to Mammy describing her life ten years after the story's end.

Drawing the Setting of the Story

Using your book as a guide, draw the setting of the story. Try to be as accurate as possible as you draw the plantation and any necessary surrounding areas.

Designing Your Own Project

If you can think of another project that will clearly demonstrate your understanding of the book, you may substitute it for one of the projects mentioned above. Talk with your teacher about this.

The Witch of Blackbird Pond

Elizabeth George Speare

When Kit's grandfather dies, she flees Barbados to go to her Aunt Rachel in America, but the austere Puritan community in Connecticut Colony soon makes her long for the life she left behind. Her one refuge in this bleak New England existence are her clandestine visits with Hannah, the witch of Blackbird Pond. When their friendship is discovered, Kit's enemies accuse her of witchcraft and are determined to see her punished.

Vocabulary	
brigantine	p. 1
pinnaces	p. 2
deadlights	p. 3
capstan	p. 3
hawser	p. 5
aft	p. 7
heathen	p. 11
nonchalance	p. 14
eke	p. 16
cowed	p. 16
punctilious	p. 17
ketch	p. 23
paduasoy	p. 41
writhe	p. 48
skeins	p. 49
popish	p. 51
pillory	p. 52
stocks	p. 52
obstreperous	p. 87
linsey-woolsey	p. 171
inveigled	p. 205

Creating a Board Game

Your book is an example of historical fiction. It is a fictitious work based on factual information. What are the historical facts surrounding the founding of Connecticut Colony, the Puritans, the Royalists, the Connecticut Charter, the witch trials, and the traffic of ships coming to Connecticut settlements? Gather information including names, dates, and places regarding these and other topics you find in your book. Place special emphasis on information about the witch trials. Create a board game with rules, markers, and a playing board. You might model your game after one with which you are familiar. Base your game on factual information, but also incorporate some fictitious information. You might choose to give players extra bonus points if they discover the untrue information. Place your complete game in an appropriately designed box. Offer opportunities for groups of students to play your game.

Routing Kit's Journey and the Slave Trade

On an enlarged version of a map of the world, locate and label the places mentioned in the book. Include Barbados, Jamaica, Antigua, the West Indies, the Connecticut River, Saybrook Harbor, Wethersfield, Boston, New Orleans, and Hartford. Chart Kit's journey on your map. Then locate information about the slave trade and the transport of rum, molasses, and slaves by ship. Place the routes used in the trade of slaves, rum, and molasses on your map. Think of a way to show how it all worked. Make it clear in your map key what information is on your map. Your final product should look like an authentic map that a ship's captain might have used in 1687.

Advertising for Colonists in America

The lives of men, women, and children colonists in Puritan Connecticut were vastly different from our lives today. New people were usually welcomed into the colony because of the work they would be able to do. Imagine that you were hired as a recruiter, and it was your job to write appealing advertisements to attract people to your colony. Write advertisements for women, men, and children in 1687. Your ads should accurately describe the jobs that are available, provide job descriptions, and list the personal qualities that are necessary for the jobs. Publish your ads in a format that might actually have been used at the time. Incorporate illustration and language style that would be typical in the 1680s.

Preparing a New England Meal

Use passages from your book and information you are able to gather to prepare a menu for a New England meal. List the ingredients needed for the items on your menu. Although some ingredients will need to be substituted for those used in 1687, try to use what the colonists originally used in the preparation of their foods. Prepare enough food so that each person will have a small taste of everything on presentation day. As you serve the meal, explain what each component is and how the preparation of your meal compares to the preparation of the meal in 1687. You may dress as a colonist and serve your meal on authentic utensils.

Reflecting the Character of Characters

In this book the author often shows two different views of the same character. Kit can appear to be vain, spoiled, unrestrained, and even witch-like, but you also see another side of her personality. She is lonely, caring, fun loving, persevering, and intelligent. Choose two characters in the book that you consider especially colorful or strong. What qualities are evident for each "side" of the characters? List the characteristics for both views of them. Think of a way to show visually or verbally (or both) the two sides of the characters. Some ideas include drawing two reflections of the character with two different sets of qualities, creating collages of the character's two views, or writing a poem for two voices. Choose your own way to present your understanding of both sides of your characters.

Constructing a Model of the Dolphin

The *Dolphin* plays an important role in the book. The author gives some description of the ship, but further research will be necessary to build a likeness of a brigantine that was capable of sailing the open seas. After you have a clear idea of what she might have looked like, construct a model of the *Dolphin*. You may use craft sticks, balsa wood, or any other appropriate materials in the construction of your model. Include small details when possible. Explain to your audience the different parts of the ship when you present your work.

Designing Your Own Project

If you can think of a project that will clearly demonstrate your understanding of the text, you may substitute it for one of the projects mentioned above. Talk with your teacher about this.

Roll of Thunder, Hear My Cry

Mildred D. Taylor

Despite night riders, burnings, and injustices that the black people of rural Mississippi suffer, the Logan family fiercely hangs on to their four hundred acres of land. Cassie and her brothers learn the price of the pride and independence that comes with owning their own place when they face losing their home and their land.

Vocabulary
meticulously . . . . p. 1
raucous . . . . p. 3
sharecropping . . . . p. 3
penchant . . . . p. 15
temerity . . . . p. 16
chignon. . . . . p. 20
imperiously. . . . . p. 22
precariously . . . . p. 49
feigned . . . . p. 56
vex . . . . p. 71
tenant . . . . p. 74
obnoxious. . . . . p. 78
promenading. . . . . p. 81
mercantile. . . . . p. 82
malevolently. . . . . p. 85
nattily . . . . p. 89
goaded . . . . p. 119
insolently . . . . p. 127
shroud. . . . . p. 171
adamant . . . . p. 203

Recreating Classrooms Then and Now

Much of what Cassie and her brothers learn about "how things are" happens at the Great Faith Elementary and Secondary School. The population, contents, buildings, and classrooms are very different than your school and classroom. Think about Mildred Taylor's descriptions in the text. Design and construct a replica of a Great Faith classroom and your classroom. Show details that make them alike and different. You may choose to make one model with two parts, or you might make two individual models. The details included in your recreation will determine how sharply the two schoolrooms contrast. Explain your comparisons on presentation day.

Investigating Segregation

Segregation is defined as "separation from others or from a main body or group." In *Roll of Thunder, Hear My Cry,* Cassie doesn't understand why black students are not allowed to ride the Jefferson Davis bus, why black and white students attend different schools, why black people are treated unfairly at the mercantile in Strawberry, and why Big Mama is sent to the back side of the market to sell her goods. From a variety of sources, find information about and examples of segregation. The history of segregation of blacks is only one example of segregation. Think of other ways segregation exists in our cities, neighborhoods, and schools. Also, how are people in the main body or group affected by segregation? In a photo essay, collage, or other visual format, show what you have learned about segregation and how it affects people in the main groups and the segregated groups. Include as many examples as you are able to find.

Surveying and Tabulating Choices

On page 97, Mama tells Cassie, "we have no choice of what color we're born or who our parents are or whether we're rich or poor. What we do have is some choice over what we make of our lives.…" Every day you make choices, and some are more important than others. The characters in your book also make choices. Keep a record of the choices they make and the consequences of their choices. Are the consequences good or bad? At the same time, keep a record of all the big and small choices you make in one day and their good and bad consequences. Survey five other people about the choices they make and the consequences of their choices. When you have gathered all your information, organize your findings formally in some way. You may choose to make a chart, a graph, a diagram, or some other format to be able to report visually and verbally what you have found out.

Writing a Poem for Two Voices

Mildred Taylor makes her characters seem alive and real with the "voices" she gives them in her book. If they could speak to you, what do you think they would say? Choose two characters from the book whose voices seem strong to you. Write a poem for their two voices that allow them to say what you think is on their minds. If you are not familiar with poems for two voices, look at two books by Paul Fleischman.

Fleischman, Paul (1985). *I Am Phoenix*. New York: Harper & Row.

_____ (1988). *Joyful Noise*. New York: Trumpet Club.

Ask a friend to practice and perform your poem with you. Sound effects, props, and dress will enhance your performance.

Making a Blueprint of the Logan Farm

The land and the family were the most important things in life to the Logans. Using descriptions from the text and your imagination, make a blueprint of the four-hundred-acre farm. Include the house, the outbuildings, and vegetation. Your plan might be a detailed drawing or a three-dimensional creation. Either way draw or make the contents according to scale so that the house, barn, cotton fields, forest, pond, roads, lawn, and Mr. Morrison's house are in correct proportion. How big is an acre? How big do you think the house and barn are? Measure to ensure the accuracy of your work. Print your labels neatly, carefully, and professionally.

Writing a Diamante

Mildred Taylor writes about justice and injustice. The Logan children know justice at home and injustice in their lives outside of their home. Find examples of justice and injustice from the text. Consider what meanings justice and injustice have for you. Write a diamante using these two opposite words or two other opposite words that have about the same meaning. A diamante is a seven-line contrast poem that is set up to appear in a diamond shape on the paper.

Line 1: one word (a noun, the subject)

Line 2: two words (adjectives describing the noun in line 1)

Line 3: three words (verbs that relate to the noun in line 1)

Line 4: four words (nouns—the first two relate to the noun in line 1, and the second two relate to the noun in line 7*)

Line 5: three words (verbs that relate to the noun in line 7)

Line 6: two words (adjectives describing the noun in line 7)

Line 7: one word (a noun opposite to the noun in line 1)

*Contrast occurs between the second and third words in this line.

Illustrate your interpretation of justice and injustice and present the illustration at the time you present your poetry.

Designing Your Own Project

If you can think of a project that will clearly demonstrate your understanding of the text, you may substitute it for one of the projects mentioned above. Talk to your teacher about this.

The Friendship

Mildred D. Taylor

Relations between the blacks and whites in post-Civil War rural Mississippi were not good. Mr. Tom Bee, a neighbor of the Logans, dared to call a white storekeeper by his first name. Many years ago Mr. Tom Bee had saved the life of the storekeeper. Their friendship, however, does not stand the test of time and race; and the Logan children witness a tragedy.

Disrespecting Others

After John Wallace shot Mr. Tom Bee, he said, "But this here disrespectin' me gotta stop and I means to stop it now." Mr. Tom Bee had again called John Wallace just by his first name. At that time in Mississippi, the white folk believed that the blacks should precede their names by "Mister" or "Missus" as a sign of respect. Times have changed since then; nowadays, different things are considered signs of disrespect. Create a chart that lists today's attitudes and actions that are a show of disrespect.

Finding a Different Way

Mr. John Wallace could have handled the situation with Mr. Tom Bee differently; he didn't have to shoot him. Rewrite the ending of the story from the point where Mr. Bee gets the tobacco and turns to leave the store. How can John Wallace "save face" in front of his sons and the other white people in the store without using his shotgun?

Researching the Civil Rights Movement

The Supreme Court case *Plessy v. Ferguson* upheld the constitutionality of "separate but equal." What exactly was this case? How did it further segregation? Research the Civil Rights Movement beginning with the Montgomery Bus Boycott in 1955 and ending with the Voting Rights Bill in 1965. What were the milestones during that ten-year period? Create a time line that indicates the results of your research. Be ready to explain the significance of the events you have chosen to place on the time line to the class.

Visualizing the Store

What does the store look like inside and out? Visualize it in your head as you reread the text. You may choose any two- or three-dimensional medium to recreate the store. Use the clues from the text to guide your project.

Designing Your Own Project

If you can think of another project that will clearly demonstrate your understanding of the book, you may substitute it for one of the projects mentioned above. Talk with your teacher about this.

📖 EMPATHY

Essential Question: What role does empathy play in the role between the reader and the writing?

Fox, Paula (1997). *Radiance Descending*. New York: Laurel Leaf.

Cisneros, Sandra (1989). *The House on Mango Street*. New York: Alfred A. Knopf.

Creech, Sharon (1995). *Walk Two Moons*. New York: HarperCollins Children's Books.

DeFelice, Cynthia (1996). *The Apprenticeship of Lucas Whittaker*. New York: Farrar, Straus & Giroux.

Frank, Anne (1959). *The Diary of a Young Girl*. New York: The American Reprint Company.

Paterson, Katherine (1991). *Lyddie*. New York: Puffin Books.

Rylant, Cynthia (1992). *Missing May*. New York: Orchard.

Yolen, Jane (1988). *The Devil's Arithmetic*. New York: Viking.

Suggested Read Alouds

Bunting, Eve (1995). *Dandelions*. New York: Harcourt Brace & Company.

_____ (1990). *The Wall*. New York: Clarion Books.

Cohen, Barbara (1983). *Molly's Pilgrim*. New York: Lothrop, Lee & Shepard.

DePaola, Tomie (1980). *Now One Foot, Now the Other*. New York: G. P. Putnam's Sons.

Fleming, Virginia (1993). *Be Kind to Eddie Lee*. New York: Philomel.

Herron, Carolivia (1997). *Nappy Hair*. New York: Alfred A. Knopf.

Lacapa, Kathleen and Michael Lacapa (1994). *Less Than Half, More Than Whole*. Flagstaff, AZ: Northland Publishing.

Maruki, Toshi (1980). *Hiroshima No Pika*. New York: Lothrop, Lee & Shepard Books.

Petersen, Jeanne Whitehouse (1994). *My Momma Sings*. New York: HarperCollins.

Thayer, Lawrence Ernest (1996). *Casey at the Bat*. New York: Atheneum Children's Books.

Thomas, Carol Joyce (1993). *Brown Honey in Broomwheat Tea*. New York: HarperCollins.

Tsuchiya, Yukio (1988). *The Faithful Elephants*. Boston: Houghton Mifflin.

Radiance Descending

Paula Fox

Jacob has Down's syndrome, and Paul has a difficult time dealing with the fact that his younger brother is different. Others don't seem to mind; in fact, other people seem to genuinely like Jacob. Are these people just pretending to like him, or do they know something that Paul doesn't?

Investigating Down's Syndrome

What is Down's syndrome? Find a way to research the condition; use the Internet, reference books, or an organization in your community. In the beginning of the book, Grandpa explains Down's syndrome to Paul in the following way. "He'll be slow…. As a rule, they're sunny children. And there's no war in them." How would you explain Down's syndrome to a young child? Create a miniplay in which one person is the "explainer" and one person is the "receiver of the explanation." Decide how old your "young child" will be. Be careful with word choice but accurate in your description at the same time.

Forgetting About Something

Paul tries to forget about Jacob. In fact, he calls it "learning to forget." Paul isn't the only character or person who tries to forget something unpleasant. Can you think of another book character or a real person who tries to forget someone or something? Create a split collage that shows on one side the world when the forgetting is accomplished, and on the other side the things that make forgetting impossible. For example, on Paul's "accomplished forgetting" side, there might be pictures of normal babies and normal young children, school buses picking up kids for school, birthday paraphernalia. The other side might contain pictures of parents, a grandfather, a smiling child, a boy waving from a window. Explain your collage to the group. Title the collage. If the character comes from a book, write the character's name, book title, and author. If the character is real, write the first name.

Describing a Secret Place

Many of us have secret places; some of them are real, and some are imaginary. Paul had his spot in the woods where he went when he wanted to "get away." Where do you go to "get away"? This could be a real location or some place where you go in your mind. Find a way to describe it. You could use words, draw a picture, build a three-dimensional model.

Planning a Birthday Party

Birthdays are special, and parties should be planned especially for the birthday person. Think about how Jacob's mother planned his party. For example, it could only last about an hour because she didn't want Jacob to tire. If you have a younger sibling, how would you plan his or her party? What would make it special? If you don't have a younger sibling, either think of a friend's brother or sister or make up an imaginary person. Create invitations for the party. Decorate the room. What games will you play? What kinds of refreshments will you have? Share your party with the rest of the class. Be sure that the party matches the birthday person.

Writing Two Poems

Paul thinks about Jacob very differently than Jacob thinks about Paul. Write two acrostic poems. Paul will write a poem about Jacob, and Jacob will write a poem about Paul. For an acrostic poem, you will write the character's name down the left side of your paper.

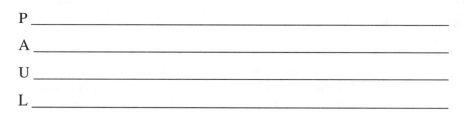

After each of the letters, write words or phrases, beginning with the letter, that describe the character. Have your poem in published form on presentation day.

Naming the Book

Talk with the members of your group about why you think Paula Fox named the book *Radiance Descending*. What does that mean? If you could rename the book, what would the title be? Create a new title for the book, and design a new cover. Be ready to explain your choice.

Designing Your Own Project

If you can think of another project that will clearly demonstrate your understanding of the book, you may substitute it for one of the projects mentioned above. Talk with your teacher about this.

The House on Mango Street

Sandra Cisneros

Esperanza Cordero is a young girl growing up in a Latino neighborhood in Chicago. In a series of vignettes, Esperanza describes her expectations for herself—expectations that are different from those the world has for her.

Describing Your House

The first vignette is titled, "House on Mango Street." The vignette doesn't talk much about the new house on Mango Street, though; it really describes the old house on Loomis. She doesn't talk too much about how the house on the third floor looks; she talks more about how she and others feel about it. Write a description of your home. Like Esperanza does, talk about feelings rather than writing an actual physical description.

Explaining Your Name

In "My Name," Esperanza tells what her name means, why and how she got the name, and what she would like her name to be. What does your name mean? How did you get your name? Would you rather have a different name? If so, what would the new name be? You may choose to display this in different ways. You could web your name (your name would be in the middle). You could write a story like Cisneros has done. You could write a poem. Choose your own way to share your information with the class.

Wanting to Be

Esperanza writes an "I want to be…." poem in the vignette "Born Bad." The following picture book is another example of a piece of "I want to be…." writing.

Moss, Thylias (1993). *I Want To Be*. New York: Dial Books for Young Readers.

Following either the style of Cisneros (poetry) or the style of Moss (picture book), create your own rendition of "I want to be…." You may be honest and truthful in your writing, or you may be fanciful. Be prepared to share with the class.

Creating a Collage

Create a collage that represents your neighborhood. The collage may be all pictures, all words, or a combination of pictures and words. You may use photographs of neighbors and places in the neighborhood; you may cut out pictures from magazines that represent your area; you may use symbols, shapes, and colors to represent the neighborhood. Try to capture the feelings that frame your small community by being careful with the design of the collage. A collage is not a hodgepodge; it is a thoughtfully constructed piece of art.

Writing the Last Vignette

Imagine that you are a grown-up Esperanza. You have left Mango Street. Where have you gone? What are you doing now? Write the final vignette for the book. Try to capture the style of the author in your writing.

Designing Your Own Project

If you can think of another project that will clearly demonstrate your understanding of the book, you may substitute it for one of the projects mentioned above. Talk with your teacher about this.

Walk Two Moons

Sharon Creech

Sal's grandparents take her to Lewiston, Idaho, where she hopes she can find her mother. On the way Sal's stories about her friend Phoebe keep Gram and Gramp entertained. The stories are funny, bittersweet, heartwarming, and lead Sal to an understanding of a range of human emotions.

Empathizing with Others

The messages thought to have been left by the potential lunatic eventually hold a great deal of significance for Sal. For example, she and Gramp take turns pretending they are walking in someone else's moccasins, and that game gives Sal new understanding about the people in her life. The same messages might apply to people and events in your life, too. For each of the four messages, keep a written record of connections you notice can be made to them in your life. As you go about your normal daily routines, be mindful about how the messages might enable you to empathize with others, much like Sal and Gramp did. You might choose to focus on one message at a time, or you could concentrate on all four simultaneously. Present your observations in a visually appealing and meaningful way. It may be necessary to change the names used in your observations to protect the privacy of others.

Writing Letters to Characters

You are able to understand how Sal feels because the author tells you what Sal is thinking. If Sal could talk to her mother, what might she say? What might Phoebe have said to her mother or vice versa? Choose two characters from the book. Speaking as first one character, write a thoughtful, meaningful, insightful letter to the other character. Then speak as the other character and write a response to the letter you receive. You can enhance your letters with doodles, illustrations, poetry, or any other tool to make your letters authentic and realistic. On the envelopes create addresses and stamps to add to their authenticity.

Mapping Characters' Lives

The lives of Sal and Phoebe have many parallels, and both characters change and develop as a result of similar circumstances. Create one map that is a visual representation of both their lives. Begin by making sequential lists of all that you learned about the two girls. Map these things separately on time lines. Decide where on your map their lives were separate or individual and where their lives come together or have things in common. Your map might look like two individual time lines that are at times parallel to one another and then meet when events bring the characters together or affect them similarly. Incorporate color, ups and downs, small illustrations, and short phrases explaining events along the way. Show the development of each character in phrases on your map.

Interviewing a Counselor

Many traumatic events take place in the lives of some of the book's characters. The loss of a child, a mother, a grandmother, or a husband are a few. Often school counselors have experience in helping others through life-altering events. Arrange for a good amount of time when you can interview your school counselor or another appropriate professional. Prepare a list of incidents in the book that strongly affected the lives of the characters. Write down pertinent questions to ask regarding these events. Take notes or use a tape recorder during your interview. Compile your information in some way. Share what you have learned on presentation day.

Representing a Character's Personality

The characters in the book have distinct personalities that can be represented visually. Create a nameplate for one of them. Measure a rectangle eighteen inches long and six inches wide on a heavy piece of paper. In tall, large letters, print their names in this space. The number of letters in the name will determine the space required for each letter. Measure so that each letter will fit evenly in the rectangle. Think about how you can form the letters in ways that represent the character's personality traits. The S in Salamanca might be made into a curving road, part of her journey with Gram and Gramp. Remember to use color, shape, and the background space to help you capture the personality of your character.

Writing a Legend or Myth

Her mother told Sal stories in the form of legends or myths from other cultures to illustrate a point. Legends and myths have heroes that perform superhuman deeds, and the stories usually have a message to teach about or explain something in life or nature. Go to a library and find books with legends or myths. Read at least three stories from them. Create your own legend or myth following the pattern you found in one of them. Illustrate your writing and cite the name of the book and the story after which your creation is modeled.

Designing Your Own Project

If you can think of a project that will clearly demonstrate your understanding of the text, you may substitute it for one of the projects mentioned above. Talk with your teacher about this.

The Apprenticeship of Lucas Whittaker

Cynthia DeFelice

Twelve-year-old Lucas Whittaker is left alone after all the members of his family die of a strange disease. Because he cannot manage the farm alone, he seeks shelter in a nearby community. A kindly doctor/dentist/barber/undertaker takes the youngster under his wing and teaches him about more than doctoring.

Vocabulary

apprenticeship	title
consumption	p. 4
afflicted	p. 4
vaguely	p. 7
sustenance	p. 9
rouse	p. 11
apothecary	p. 20
appraisingly	p. 22
vermin	p. 23
hearth	p. 26
ravages	p. 27
scant	p. 28
miserly	p. 29
confounded	p. 45
efficacious	p. 52
ebullience	p. 54
purge	p. 56
persnickety	p. 62
cauterize	p. 68
putrefaction	p. 68
exhilarated	p. 80
frigid	p. 91
melancholy	p. 106
pungent	p. 121

Curing Diseases

During the mid-1850s, there were several often-fatal diseases such as "consumption" that we since have found ways to prevent or cure. The author talks about the inoculation for smallpox in the story. What other diseases were prevalent then that are no longer widespread because of preventative measures or cures? Create a chart that lists the disease, the preventative measure or cure, the discoverer, and the date of discovery. Make a second list that describes diseases that we still have not been able to cure or prevent.

Creating a Book of Herbal Medicines

Moll Garfield knew a great deal about natural remedies; she used herbs, roots, stalks, and bulbs of plants to heal the body and the spirit. Research herbal medicines and create a book that indicates your findings. Each page should contain the name of the herb, a picture of it (if you can actually find the herb, you might want to press it and affix it to the page), the use for the herb, and how to prepare the herb for usage. You may include herbal cures that were used during the time the book took place as well as herbs that are used today.

Comparing Twelve-Year-Old Boys of 1850 with Twelve-Year-Old Boys of Today

Create some kind of graphic organizer (maybe a Venn diagram or another kind of organizer you can create on the computer) in which you can compare a twelve-year-old boy from 1850 with a twelve-year-old boy today. Some questions you might explore are

> What are the boy's responsibilities?
> What does the boy do for recreation or fun?
> How does the boy treat his elders?
> How is the education similar? Different?

Picturing Lucas Whittaker

Cynthia DeFelice doesn't give a detailed physical description of Lucas Whittaker. What do you think he looked like? Describe him in words, and then create a picture of him. You may generate the picture with the computer, cut pictures out of magazines, draw the picture, or create a three-dimensional sculpture.

Embalming

Find the descriptions in the book where the bodies were dug up. How were the bodies embalmed in 1850? How are they embalmed today? How do you think they will be embalmed in 150 years? What are your reasons for your predictions?

Keeping Things That Matter

When Lucas returned from his visit home, he brought back treasured family objects: the patchwork quilt his mother had made, his father's gold pocket watch and chain, his mother's Bible, a book of poetry, a silver birth cup of Lizy's, and the small cloth bag with the four coins inside. What family objects would you put in a "treasure bag"? Lucas used the quilt for his "bag." What would your bag be made from? Bring your "treasure bag" on presentation day and share your family objects with the class. Be able to explain your choices.

Designing Your Own Project

If you can think of another project that will clearly demonstrate your understanding of the book, you may substitute it for one of the projects mentioned above. Talk with your teacher about this.

The Diary of a Young Girl

Anne Frank

Anne Frank kept a diary while she and her family were in hiding during the German occupation of Holland during World War II. The diary was only found after the family was discovered and sent to a concentration camp. Anne's day-to-day narration about life in the "Secret Annexe" gives the world a clear view of what it was to like to be young, Jewish, and a captive of circumstances.

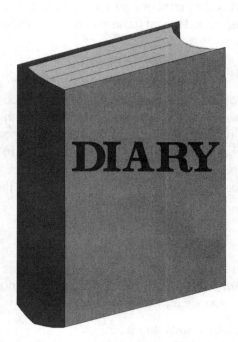

Vocabulary	
witticisms	p. 142
furbelows	p. 142
scoffingly	p. 159
cribbing	p. 160
superficial	p. 161
despondency	p. 162
embryonic	p. 162
nonchalance	p. 164
adroit	p. 169
sallies	p. 175
blithely	p. 178
variegated	p. 190
jocular	p. 200
unadulterated	p. 227

Mapping Changes in Anne's Character

Anne speaks of changes in herself on page 161. What might have caused some of these changes in her? Create a life map showing events or situations that might have initiated changes in Anne's thinking and attitudes. After each section on your map, create a stopping or changing place. With each "stop" on the map, include a short explanation about what causes a change in Anne and what the change actually is. Show in some visual way if you think the change was better for Anne or worse for her. Incorporate some illustration and color in your map to lend importance to events and to create visual interest.

Presenting the Nazi Occupation of Holland

Find information about the Nazi occupation of Holland during World War II. Why were the Jews marked for persecution and extinction? What prompted some of the citizens to defy German laws and protect some Jews? What was the role of the Dutch Green Police? Prepare a written, visual, and verbal presentation of the information you have gathered about the events and persons during this time period. Your presentation will provide the backdrop for the story about Anne and her fellow prisoners. It will set the tone for the rest of your group's presentation.

Constructing a Replica of the "Secret Annexe"

Using data collected while reading the book, construct a replica of the hiding place and its contents. When you furnish the annexe, recreate as authentically as possible the furniture, linens, food, clothing, people, and any other things that might have been in the rooms.

Representing Influential Characters in Anne's Life

There are eight persons hidden in the "Secret Annexe." Besides Anne, who do you think are the most influential persons she writes about in her diary? They could be positive or negative influences. Who elicits the strongest reactions from you? Choose three characters and visually represent their most outstanding characteristics. Remember that individuals are very complex, and each character has multiple facets. You may need to show more than one view of the characters to represent them fully.

Recreating Pivotal Scenes from the Diary

As you read Anne's diary, certain scenes might seem more important to you than others. Choose at least five scenes that you think have the most impact on the story or the characters. Consider the setting, the characters, and the situations depicted in the scenes. Prepare a series of tableaux with actors and props to recreate what you think are the turning points in the story. A tableau is a frozen picture with real actors in positions that capture for the audience the strongest moment in a scene. You may choose actors to recreate the scenes, and you need a narrator to explain the importance of the situation.

Writing an I Am Poem

Anne writes poignantly about herself and her observations of others. Imagine that you are one of the characters in the book. Write an *I Am* poem describing your innermost thoughts, fears, and dreams. The form for the poem will help you speak for your character.

I am (two special characteristics you have)
I wonder (something you're actually curious about)
I hear (an imaginary sound)
I want (an actual desire)
I am (the first line of the poem repeated)

I pretend (something you pretend to do)
I feel (a feeling about something imaginary)
I touch (an imaginary touch)
I worry (something that really bothers you)
I cry (something that makes you very sad)
I am (the first line of the poem repeated)

I understand (something you know is true)
I say (something you believe in)
I dream (something you actually dream about)
I try (something you really make an effort about)
I hope (something you actually hope for)
I am (the first line of the poem repeated)

Designing Your Own Project

If you can think of a project that will clearly demonstrate your understanding of the text, you may substitute it for one of the projects mentioned above. Talk with your teacher about this.

Lyddie

Katherine Paterson

The story begins in Vermont in the year of 1843. Father has gone in search of riches, and Mama has gone a bit crazy. Mama takes the youngest children to live with her sister and brother-in-law, while Lyddie and Charlie remain alone on the farm. Finally, Mama apprentices both of her older children to work for their way in life. Lyddie, after being "let go" from her servitude at the inn, finds herself in the mills in Lowell, Massachusetts. How does a mere child survive such harsh conditions? How does a child thrive in these conditions?

Vocabulary
adversary . . . . p. 4
specter . . . . p. 6
noxious . . . . p. 13
fugitive . . . . p. 40
veritable . . . . p. 42
impertinent . . . . p. 44
rivulets . . . . p. 47
alight. . . . . p. 49
irate. . . . . p. 50
pate. . . . . p. 63
raucous . . . . p. 75
feigning . . . . p. 82
indefatigable. . . . . p. 86
rapier . . . . p. 87
scrupulous . . . . p. 155
paragon. . . . . p. 157
conundrum . . . . p. 160
turpitude . . . . p. 167

Researching the Mills in Lowell, Massachusetts, and the Child Labor Laws

What can you find out about the textile mills in Lowell? The mills really did exist. Did they exploit child labor? When did the child labor laws come into existence? What happened to the mills when child labor was no longer allowed?

Writing a Letter to the Mill Owner

Imagine that you have just been released from the mill, as Lyddie was. You, too, were not given a certificate. Instead of going back home, you have decided to fight the decision. You begin by writing a letter to the head of the company. What will you say? You know that you need to be temperate and calm but exact in your writing.

Comparing the Characters

Lyddie's favorite book is *Oliver Twist* by Charles Dickens. The book has been made into a stage play and a movie. Either read the story or watch the movie. How are the characters of Oliver and Lyddie similar? Using Paul Fleischman's *Joyful Noise: Poems for Two Voices* as a guide, write a poem for Lyddie and Oliver that shows how they are different and similar. Are there any other characters in the two books that seem similar? What about Fagin and Mr. Marsden?

Creating an Image of Ezekial

After Lyddie meets Ezekial, she buys two books: *Narrative of the Life of Frederick Douglass: An American Slave Written by Himself* and a Bible. Both books remind her of Ezekial. Lyddie likes to read the Psalms. As she read both, "she could hear Ezekial's rich, warm voice filling the darkness of the cabin." Create an image of Ezekial. You may draw him, create a collage or a clay model, or make anything else that will represent his personage.

Missing Luke Stevens

The book ends with the words, " 'We can still hop, Luke Stevens,' Lyddie said, 'but not aloud.' " What do you think Lyddie intends to do? Will she go to Oberlin College in Ohio? Will she stay in Vermont and marry Luke? Will she buy back the cabin and her family's land and live there alone? Write a final chapter to the book describing what happens to Lyddie. Try to keep the writing in the style of Katherine Paterson.

Writing Historical Fiction

Many authors (Katherine Paterson is one) write historical fiction. Their stories are based on events that really happened; the characters are often fictional. If you were going to write a historical fiction book, what are some topics from which you could choose? Make a list of these topics. Next, choose your favorite and create some fictional characters to go with the topic. Describe your characters in words first, then create or find pictures that match the descriptions. Finally, where will your story be set? Why will it take place there? Make some kind of chart that details your chosen topic, the characters who will tell your story, and the story's setting.

Designing Your Own Project

If you can think of another project that will clearly demonstrate your understanding of the book, you may substitute it for one of the projects mentioned above. Talk with your teacher about this.

Missing May

Cynthia Rylant

Twelve-year-old Summer and her elderly foster father, Ob, mourn the death of her foster mother, May. With the help of Summer's somewhat "strange" classmate Cletus, Summer and Ob deal with May's passing. The novel teaches about death and grief, helps students to understand and communicate better with the elderly, and assists young people in knowing how and when to listen rather than speak.

Vocabulary	
hoisted	p. 5
whirligig	p. 6
grim	p. 10
stupefaction	p. 12
collaborate	p. 19
enthralled	p. 22
surreal	p. 26
suffragettes	p. 28
bereavement	p. 29
delirium	p. 34
consoler	p. 36
infernal	p. 43
exhilarated	p. 49
hoax	p. 56
flabbergasted	p. 63
traipsing	p. 74

Creating Word Pictures

Rylant's descriptions create vivid pictures in our minds. She describes the capitol building of West Virginia by saying, "The capitol building sprawled gray concrete like a regal queen spreading out her petticoats, and its giant dome glittered pure gold in the morning sun." Draw this description. Don't draw the capitol building as you may have seen pictures of it; draw the author's description of it. Put the quote from the text somewhere on the page. Don't forget to use quotation marks. Find other descriptions in the book and illustrate those also.

Giving Clever Names

The Reverend Miriam B. Young is called "Small Medium at Large" or the "Bat Lady." Ob tells Cletus that after their trip, he might be called a "Rent-a-Séance Man." The names are representative of who the characters are and what they do. What names can you create for May, Summer, Ob, Cletus's mother and father, and any other characters in the book.

Designing and Building Whirligigs

Ob is a designer and builder of whirligigs. His are no ordinary whirligigs, though. "They were *The Mysteries*.... There was Fire and Love and Dreams and Death." Design and build your own mysterious whirligig. Be sure to give it a title.

Assembling a Terrarium

May's garden holds beloved and practical plants. Make a terrarium and place in it plants that are both "beloved" and "practical" to you. Why are some plants beloved or practical and others aren't? What characteristics do your plants have in common? Write a list of the plants you will put in your terrarium. List the Latin name and the common name for each. Learn the soil, light, and water requirements of the plants you choose. Gardening books can help you with the names and the requirements. An old aquarium makes a good container for a terrarium. Be sure to cover the aquarium in some way.

Writing Your Own Picture Book

Read two picture books by Cynthia Rylant: *When I Was Young in the Mountains* and *The Relatives Came*. Write and illustrate your own children's story that tells a story similar to one of those told by Rylant. Be sure to set up the book in the correct format. Be prepared to share your book on presentation day. The following book will give you a good model:

Aliki (1986). *How a Book Is Made*. New York: Trumpet Club.

Designing Your Own Project

If you can think of another project that will clearly demonstrate your understanding of the book, you may substitute it for one of the projects mentioned above. Talk with your teacher about this.

The Devil's Arithmetic

Jane Yolen

When Hannah opens the door during Passover Seder, she suddenly finds herself in the unfamiliar world of a Polish village in the 1940s. Hannah had grown tired of listening to her relatives tell stories about the Holocaust, but now she finds herself in a terrifying situation. The Nazi soldiers are taking the villagers away, and only Hannah knows where they are going.

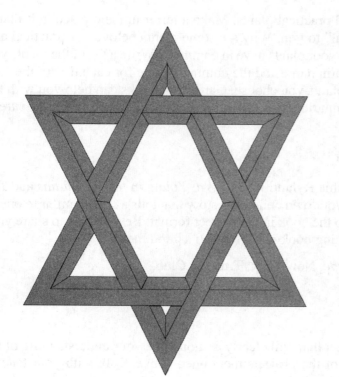

Vocabulary	
unleavened	p. 5
yarzeit	p. 12
Haggadah	p. 13
yarmulke	p. 14
cloying	p. 16
afikoman	p. 16
matzoh	p. 16
kosher	p. 17
rabbi	p. 17
Chanukah	p. 18
Elijah	p. 19
shadchan	p. 20
shtetl	p. 26
Yiddish	p. 28
Torah	p. 29
schnorrers	p. 38
yeshiva bocher	p. 39
shmatte	p. 42
shul	p. 43
rendar	p. 45
goy	p. 47
mishigaas	p. 48
klezmer	p. 52
badchan	p. 54
shadchan	p. 54
Sherele	p. 59
synagogue	p. 62
malach ha-mavis	p. 62
bobbe meinses	p. 67
creamatoria	p. 72

Giving Meaning to Characters' Stories

Rivka says, "We all have such stories. It is a brutal arithmetic.... This is my authority." Rivka's story is the letters and numbers on her tattooed arm. Choose five other characters from the book. Create a tattoo for each of them, and give each character a story. Some story parts might be from the book itself. Other parts might be from your perceptions about the characters. Display your stories in some way. You might even ask your audience to match the stories to the characters.

Remembering the Devil's Arithmetic

Hannah's mission is to remember everything she has seen and experienced. Rivka has taught her, "as long as we can remember, all those gone before are alive inside us." The Holocaust Museum in Washington, D.C., for example, was created to help people remember. If you were Hannah, Aunt Eva, or another camp survivor, how would you tell the world about all you remember? Decide on a way you could do your part in reminding the world about the Holocaust. Put your memories in a context of your choosing to help everyone understand the immensity of your experiences and remember those gone before you.

Thinking About Being Thankful

The hardships of life in the camp make Chaya realize that she did not appreciate many things in her life: the blue dress she hated, foods she didn't like, and even something as simple as having hair because "without their hair, all the women looked the same." In the camp, she wishes she could have all these things. There are things in your life that you might complain about, take for granted, or don't give much thought to, but you might miss these things if they were gone. Write down the things that Chaya misses now that she can no longer have them. List some of the things that are either a nuisance or something you dislike. Think about how many of these things on your list you would suddenly appreciate if they were taken away from you. Think about people and opportunities as well as things and activities. When you have your ideas organized, create a collage or other visual representation that illustrates your thoughts about being grateful and thankful.

Authoring and Performing a Play

Israel became a place of refuge for surviving Jews after World War II. In the book Chaya urges the group from Viosk to run away there, but no one even knows a place like that exists. Find information about the founding of Israel. Write the script for a play, continuing the story about those who were alive at the end of the book, their decision to go to Israel, their journey, and their arrival at their new home. The Epilogue will help with ideas to get you started. Hold tryouts for the cast of your play. Perform your play using props, dressing appropriately, and staging the setting.

Finding the Meaning of Hebrew and Yiddish Words

The vocabulary words would be familiar to someone who knows about Jewish customs and culture. Interview a rabbi or another person who could help you understand and define these terms. You might call a Jewish synagogue in your area to arrange your interview. After you have gathered your information, find a way to publish what you have learned. You might choose to make an illustrated book, or you might choose to display your information visually in some way.

Mapping German-Occupied Europe

At the beginning of and during World War II, Germany invaded and occupied many European countries. Wherever the Nazis took over, Jews were persecuted. Hitler, Germany's Nazi leader, devised the Final Solution to murder Jewish and "undesirable" people. Find out what countries the German army controlled. Create and label a map that encompasses all of these countries and the surrounding areas. Include Viosk, Poland, and the Auschwitz and Treblinka concentration camps. Incorporate color, shading, illustration, and three-dimensional features to make your map exciting and representative of events in the book.

Designing Your Own Project

If you can think of a project that will clearly demonstrate your understanding of the text, you may substitute it for one of the projects mentioned above. Talk with your teacher about this.

📖COURAGE AND SURVIVAL

Essential Question: How do events in a book influence a character's growth?

Curtis, Christopher Paul (1999). *Bud, Not Buddy*. New York: Delacorte Press.

Cushman, Karen (1995). *The Midwife's Apprentice*. New York: HarperCollins.

Fleischman, Paul (1997). *Seedfolks*. New York: HarperCollins Children's Books.

Hansen, Joyce (1988). *Out from This Place*. New York: Avon Books.

Sachar, Louis (1998). *Holes*. New York: Farrar, Straus & Giroux.

Sperry, Armstrong (1940). *Call It Courage*. New York: Macmillan.

White, Ruth (1996). *Belle Prater's Boy*. New York: HarperCollins.

Yep, Laurence (1994). *Dragon's Gate*. New York: HarperTrophy.

Suggested Read Alouds

Bunting, Eve (1989). *The Wednesday Surprise*. New York: Clarion Books.

_____ (1998). *Your Move*. Singapore: Harcourt Brace.

Innocenti, Roberto (1985). *Rose Blanche*. Mankato, MN: Creative Education.

Longfellow, Henry Wadsworth (1990). *Paul Revere's Ride*. New York: Dutton Children's Books.

Mayer, Marianna (1995). *Turandot*. New York: William Morrow.

Siebert, Diane (1991). *Sierra*. New York: HarperCollins.

Service, Robert W. (1987). *The Cremation of Sam McGee*. New York: Greenwillow Books.

Turner, Ann (1985). *Dakota Dugout*. New York: Macmillan.

Seedfolks

Paul Fleischman

How do people survive in an inner-city neighborhood? Thirteen characters, led by a young girl, take a chance and do something that hasn't been done before in their neighborhood. Strangers come together and, because they have courage and faith, transform an empty lot into a lush garden that feeds not only their bellies but also their souls.

Mapping the Countries of Origin

Each of the characters in the story comes from a different place around the world. Find a large world map, and mark each character's country of origin. Either draw a line from that country to Cleveland, Ohio, or extend a string from the country of origin to Cleveland.

Plotting a Garden

Imagine that you have been given a piece of land that is 100 feet by 200 feet. Create a scale drawing that shows your land. Don't forget to provide a key that explains the scale. Divide your land into ten equal parts. One of the parts will be yours, and you may give the other nine parts to nine people you know. To whom will you give your parcels of land? What will they grow in their garden and why? Think about the characters in the book; each of them chose to grow a particular crop for a particular reason. Fill in the areas of your scale drawing with the appropriate crops. Be ready to explain your reasoning to the class.

Charting the Struggles

Each of the thirteen characters resolves some kind of conflict by planting a plot in the garden. Create a chart with three columns. The first column will contain the character's name; the second will describe the conflict; and the third will tell how the conflict is resolved.

Creating the Fourteenth Character

Imagine that there is one plot in the garden that no one has claimed. Create a character who lives in the Cleveland neighborhood. As the author has done in the previous chapters, tell the character's country of origin, his or her conflict, and how she or he resolves the conflict. What does this person plant in the garden? Why? Also, how does your new character interact with the other thirteen characters?

Making a Character Collage

What do the thirteen (or fourteen) characters look like? The author describes them to some degree. Can you see them "in your mind's eye"? Using either pictures cut from magazines or your own drawings, create a collage that contains pictures of each of the characters. Be careful of placement in the collage. Try to show relationships among them by how you place them on the paper.

Assembling a Terrarium

Imagine that a terrarium is your plot in the garden. What will you plant and why? How much sunlight does your plant(s) require? How much water will you need to give it? An aquarium makes a good container for a terrarium, or, for a smaller terrarium, you could use a clean, two-liter plastic bottle. To do this, cut the bottom portion of the plastic bottle right above the dark area. Place the charcoal, soil, and plants in the bottom portion of the bottle and replace the top of the bottle, keeping the lid screwed on the top. If you choose to use an aquarium or an old fish bowl, be sure to cover it in some way.

Designing Your Own Project

If you can think of another project that will clearly demonstrate your understanding of the book, you may substitute it for one of the other projects. Talk with your teacher about this.

Bud, Not Buddy

Christopher Paul Curtis

Bud is ten years old. His mother died when he was six, before she ever told him who his father was. Since she died, Bud has been living in a series of foster homes or in "the Home." He decides it's time to find his father (his mother did leave him a clue). His travels take him from Flint to Grand Rapids, both of which are towns in Michigan. He doesn't find his father, but he finds someone almost as good.

Vocabulary
commence . . . . p. 5
devastators . . . . p. 7
welted . . . . p. 11
lavatory . . . . p. 11
urchin . . . . p. 12
ringworm . . . . p. 41
lice . . . . p. 41
tetters . . . . p. 41
matrimonial . . . . p. 56
genie . . . . p. 82
flimsy . . . . p. 131
craw . . . . p. 160

Comparing the Depression to Today

The story takes place in 1936 during the Great Depression. Use the Internet or go to the library and find out about the Depression. Why did it happen? What was it? What was life like during that time? Use a Venn diagram to show the differences and the similarities between life during the Depression and life today. Think of universals of culture as you conduct your research: food, clothing, shelter, geography, technology, religion, education, government, economy, customs, and celebrations.

Writing Rules for Living

Bud Caldwell's Rules and Things for Having a Funner Life and Making a Better Liar Out of Yourself pop up throughout the book. Bud says that his rules keep him from making the same mistakes seven or eight times. What rules do you and your group members have that keep you from making the same mistakes time after time? Do your parents have these kinds of rules? What would you call your rules? Create a chart that lists your rules for living.

Creating Nicknames

The members of the Dusky Devastators of the Depression all had nicknames. Collect pictures of some of your friends and display them in some kind of creative way. You might exhibit them on some kind of poster, in a photo album, in a book, or on paperdoll-type cutouts. Each of your friends should have a nickname. What names will you choose for each of them? Why will you choose those names? You might want to refer to the end of Chapter 16 to see how Bud got his nickname.

Writing a Poem for Two Voices

If you are not familiar with poems for two voices, look at two books by Paul Fleischman.

Fleischman, Paul (1985). *I Am Phoenix*. New York: Harper & Row.

_____ (1988). *Joyful Noise*. New York: Trumpet Club.

Bud is almost like two different people at the beginning and end of the story. Create a poem for two voices, using the format Fleischman created, about Bud's feelings in the beginning of the book and his feelings at the end of the book. After you have written it, practice it with a group member in preparation for presenting it to the class.

Playing Music of the Era

Find some music that was popular during the Depression. Listen carefully to it. Are there similarities between the popular pieces? How is the mood of the times portrayed through the music? Find one that you think is representative of the music of the times and play it for the class. Point out how this particular piece captures the mood and feelings of the time.

Interviewing J. Edgar Hoover

Who was J. Edgar Hoover? Why was he important during the Depression? What did he do for the population of the United States? Imagine that you are a talk show host (radio—American families did not have televisions at the time), and J. Edgar Hoover will be your guest. One of the group members should play the part of Hoover. Introduce your guest (you may want to play appropriate music) and have an in-depth conversation with him. You'll have to script your questions and answers carefully. You and Hoover should both dress as authentically as possible. Present your interview to the class.

Designing Your Own Project

If you can think of another project that will clearly demonstrate your understanding of the text, you may substitute it for one of the projects mentioned above. Talk with your teacher about this.

The Midwife's Apprentice

Karen Cushman

Brat, a girl with no home, no parents, and no name, crawls into a farmer's dung heap to find shelter and warmth. The next morning she emerges from the refuse like a dung beetle. Hence, her new name, Beetle. One of the first persons she sees is Jane the Midwife who sees an opportunity to get work from a starved urchin in exchange for a little food. So begins Beetle's new career as a midwife's apprentice. It's a hard life, but in time she earns a new name and a place for herself in the world.

Vocabulary

Giving Meaning to Names

The main character, Alyce, underwent many changes from your first introduction to her as Brat to the person she eventually becomes at the end of the book. Her personality changes parallel her name changes. The names Brat, Beetle, Alyce, and Midwife are the names the author uses for her. You might have more ideas for names that were not included in the author's writing (such as Provider). Using at least four names for her character, write a series of acrostic poems that communicate your understanding of how Alyce changed throughout the book. Each line of each of your poems needs to begin with a word or phrase that matches the letters of the name and that is descriptive of the character at the time the name was used in the book.

Investigating Midwifery and Interviewing a Midwife

The Author's Note at the end of the book gives you some information about midwifery. Go to other sources to get more information about midwifery during medieval times and midwifery in the present time. Include a primary-source interview with a practicing midwife in your town. Be sure to prepare thoughtful questions to ask during your interview. In what ways is midwifery different today than from medieval times? How have practices changed? Who might become a midwife today? Local hospitals frequently employ midwives in the obstetric departments. The yellow pages may help you find names and places. Gather and organize your information to present in some way. You might choose to use a newspaper, newscast, report, video, PowerPoint, or other format.

Building a Medieval Village

Beetle finds kindness and acceptance in the village of Gobnet-Under-Green. It is here where she takes the name Alyce. Using the descriptions in the book, construct an authentic medieval village. Include homes and shops mentioned in the book. Your construction needs to be three-dimensional with rich details in the village and the surrounding countryside. Include signs for shops, and label the places you read about. Use materials and art media of your choice.

Packing a Medicine Bag

In a midwife's medicine bag were the potions and concoctions she had prepared to help her ease the pain of childbearing and to successfully deliver babies. Many of these preparations consisted of herbs and other plants she found around her village. Some were mixtures of various animal parts. The author describes these ingredients throughout the book. Make an authentic bag or kit and pack it with what Jane or Alyce might have had in their medicine bags. Each item needs to have a label that describes what it is and how it is used. Of course, you can substitute ingredients for what you think the authentic contents might look like.

Preparing a Midwifery License

Who makes a better midwife, Jane or Alyce? Why do you think this? Jane has certain desirable skills, and Alyce is competent in other areas. What do you think should be the requirements for a good midwife? What do you think are the qualities, skills, education, and experience that should be necessary for a person to be a licensed midwife? What would be the qualifications for being a good midwife? You might want to survey your classmates for ideas. Design a Midwifery License that has an official appearance and that has qualifications and requirements for the job clearly stated.

Mapping Character Traits

Major events in the book shaped Alyce's life. What were the turning points in her life, and how did they affect her? Think about how Alyce's character changed and what happened to make these changes occur. Consider how she "grew" as a person and what character traits she developed. Create a map of her life that represents the events and changes that occurred. Use color and size to enhance your ideas. Your map can be one dimensional or multidimensional.

Designing Your Own Project

If you can think of another project that will clearly demonstrate your understanding of the book, you may substitute it for one of the projects mentioned above. Talk with your teacher about this.

Out from This Place

Joyce Hansen

This book is based on actual events that happened at the end of the Civil War. Easter and her friends Obi and Jason went to the islands off the South Carolina coast and worked for wages on the plantations that the Union army controlled. The story documents Easter's (she was an Easter gift to her mistress) search for freedom, education, belonging, and love.

Vocabulary	
fugitives	p. 33
dilapidated	p. 35
twinge	p. 51
bolls	p. 65
bondage	p. 72
courier	p. 110
insurrection	p. 111
amends	p. 115
condolences	p. 117
sojourn	p. 119

Researching New Canaan

New Canaan, the community described in *Out from This Place* is based on an actual South Carolina island community that was developed after the Civil War. Using the Internet or library resources, find out about these island developments. How were the towns built? Who built them? What kinds of people occupied them? What did they do for a living? Prepare a report that details the building of one of the towns.

Living in New Canaan

Imagine that you are one of the people who plans and then builds one of the South Carolina island towns. Write a journal that details your feelings as the town in being planned and then built. You will have to create your own character. Are you man or woman? Child or adult? Black or white? Be sure that, through your journal entries, you introduce and describe your character. Date your entries. Be sure that you go through the entire cycle in your journal.

Comparing Flora and Fauna

Coastal South Carolina is a temperate, humid climate. The trees, plants, shrubs, flowers, and grasses that grow there are peculiar to that geographic location. Many species of growing things are described in the book. Page 35, for example, mentions marsh elder, salt myrtle, Spanish moss, magnolia, and dogwood. Find pictures and descriptions of these plants. How are they alike or different from the plants that grow in your climate or geographic area? Create a "split mural" where one side shows the coastal South Carolina plants, and the other side shows the plants of your area.

Writing a Second Epilogue

Imagine Obi walking into the Freedman's Bureau in Charleston. What happens? Using the style and the tone of the text, write another epilogue to the book. Does Obi find Easter? How does he find her? Where does he find her? What happens to Jason? Think of all the unanswered questions you have and answer them in your epilogue.

Weaving a Mat

Easter and the younger girls weave mats from grasses and palmetto fronds. Most world cultures have woven articles for home use. What could you weave with native plants in your area? Weave a mat or a basket or some other useful, home item. If you can't find native plants, get something at your local craft store to use for weaving.

Learning to Read

There are many books that describe learning to read. *Lyddie* by Katherine Paterson and *Nightjohn* by Gary Paulsen are two of these books. Why is reading so important? Write a definition poem titled "Reading is _____." In your poem (remember that poetry does not have to rhyme), explain what reading enables people to do that they couldn't do if they were unable to read. You may do this in your own voice or in the voice of a character from one of the many books that describes the process of learning to read.

Designing Your Own Project

If you can think of another project that will clearly demonstrate your understanding of the book, you may substitute it for one of the projects mentioned above. Talk with your teacher about this.

Holes

Louis Sachar

Camp Green Lake is a camp for bad boys. Stanley Yelnats isn't a bad boy; he's just a boy who was in the wrong place at the wrong time. At Camp Green Lake, the bad boys dig holes. The digging is supposed to improve their character, but Stanley knows that there must be more to it than that. As the pieces of the story puzzle fit together, the mystery unravels. Stanley, a shy and uncourageous boy who comes from a family plagued by bad luck, survives Camp Green Lake and learns about himself and his family in the process.

Vocabulary	
perseverance	p. 8
premises	p. 12
spigot	p. 20
coincidence	p. 24
reluctantly	p. 34
grimaced	p. 39
gash	p. 78
recede	p. 91
spewed	p. 103
concoctions	p. 108
parched	p. 157
gloppier	p. 171
rigid	p. 210
delirium	p. 215

Mapping the Area

Using clues from the text, create a map of Camp Green Lake and the surrounding area as it exists during the stay of Stanley and the other boys. The map can be drawn or constructed three-dimensionally. Include any flora and fauna in the area. Also include the animal life that is mentioned in the story. Green Lake was a different place during the time of Dr. Hawthorn, Sam, the onion man, and Katherine Barlow. You'll find this story mainly in Chapters 25 and 26. Create a map (drawn or three-dimensional) of the Green Lake area that existed 110 years ago. Be sure to show the differences between "then" and "now." Are there similarities? If so, show these, too. Be ready to explain both your maps to the class.

Creating a Character Life Map

At the beginning of the book, the Stanley who arrived at Camp Green Lake was a very different boy from the one who left Camp Green Lake. Make a map of his life as we know it from the story. It should illustrate his progress from the "fat boy with no friends" to a leader among the boys at the camp. A life map is like a road map. The stops along the way represent memorable or significant events from the character's life. The curves and turns on the map represent good or bad times, big or small changes. You will want to use a combination of pictures and well-worded phrases to describe the events in Stanley's life; there is no need for long sentences.

Choosing Appropriate Nicknames

The boys at Camp Green Lake have interesting nicknames. Are the names appropriate? Find a well-known children's story or fairy tale and think of nicknames that the characters might have. Rewrite it using nicknames rather than the names given in the story. Practice telling your story aloud. Present it to the class and see if they can guess what story you're telling.

Becoming the Characters

What do Zero, Zigzag, X-ray, and the others look like? Determine from clues within the text how the characters look, how they dress, and how they act when they're together. Act out a short scene from the book.

Finding Palindromes

The name Stanley Yelnats is a palindrome. A palindrome is a word or sentence that reads the same backward and forward. "Madam, I'm Adam" is another palindrome. "Mom," "Dad," and "Pop" are also palindromes. What are some others? Can you think of sentences or phrases as well as one-word palindromes. Create a chart that displays your palindromes for the class to see.

Changing a Song

The "pig" lullaby threads its way through the book, adding both consistency and continuity. Using either yourself or another literary character as the example, choose a well-known tune and rewrite the lyrics to demonstrate both consistency and continuity through the story of life. Practice singing your new song, and present it to the class. Be ready to tell why you wrote the lyrics as you did.

Challenging Curses

"Stanley's mother insists that there never was a curse." Can you think of other curses that exist, either in real life or in literature? For instance, will you really have seven years bad luck if you break a mirror? After you locate some curses, find out where they originated and why people believed that they were true. A good place to begin might be with the myths that surround "La Llorona." After you've done the research, a good way to present your research might be a debate between the "believers" and the "nonbelievers." Try to convince the audience that the curses you've chosen to talk about either are or are not true.

Designing Your Own Project

If you can think of a project that will clearly demonstrate your understanding of the text, you may substitute it for one of the projects mentioned above. Talk with your teacher about this.

Call It Courage

Armstrong Sperry

When he was a small boy, Mafatu nearly drowned at sea. Since then he has been terrified of the ocean. Unable to conquer his fear of the water, he remains on the island doing "women's work" while the other boys venture out beyond the barrier reef. Finally, driven from the island by the scorn and indifference of his peers and his father, Mafatu flees Hikueru in shame. He knows the time has come to face Moana, the god of the sea. With only his small dog Uri for company, Mafatu sails out alone to die or to prove his courage.

Vocabulary	
indifference	p. 1
barrier reef	p. 3
frigate	p. 3
outrigger	p. 3
thwarts	p. 3
jibes	p. 6
albatross	p. 7
bonitos	p. 8
lagoon	p. 12
atoll	p. 14
ballast	p. 16
tumult	p. 19
slewed	p. 19
luminous	p. 22
caustic	p. 32
ramparts	p. 35
adze	p. 37
irresolute	p. 40
congealed	p. 41
breadfruit	p. 46
plaited	p. 49
hitch	p. 71
phosphorescent	p. 74
zephyr	p. 82

Locating the Island

There are 30,000 islands in the Pacific Ocean. Many of these lie in curved rows called archipelagos. Others are isolated peaks that are really ocean mountaintops. The Pacific Ocean islands lying east of the international date line are called the Polynesian Islands, meaning "many islands." French Polynesia is in this group, and the Tuamotu Archipelago is located there. It is located approximately 10 to 20 degrees south and 135 to 150 degrees west on a world map. Consult an atlas to find the location of the setting of the book. Why do you think Mafatu expected to reach Tahiti? On which of the nearby islands do you think he actually landed? Draw, build, or construct a map of this part of the world. Label the important geographic locations and features. Indicate the route you think Mafatu took. Also, go to the library and find information about the Polynesian islanders. On presentation day talk about the inhabitants of and geographic features in this part of the world.

Constructing Relief Maps

The Polynesian Islands are in an area shaped like a triangle. Most are tops of volcanic mountains, but some are mounds of sand on a reef that surrounds a shallow lagoon. This kind of island is an atoll. Construct two relief maps out of clay, papier-mâché, salt dough, or other medium. Make one map of Hikueru and the other of the island where the sea took Mafatu. On each map show the island itself, its prominent features, and the surrounding water. Include details that represent events in your book.

Creating a Collage of Good and Evil

Armstrong Sperry creates strong images of what represents good and what represents evil in Mafatu's life. These images can be either concrete (something that can be touched) or abstract (something that is felt or understood). For example, the tiger shark might be perceived as evil and is concrete. Mafatu's fear of the sea might also be thought of as evil and is abstract. Create a collage of visual or tactile objects that represent the good things and the evil things in Mafatu's life. Think about how you will organize your ideas. They need to be visually clear. You should be able to explain your ideas clearly on presentation day.

Writing a Color Poem

If you need some ideas for writing a color poem, look at this book.

O'Neill, Mary (1961). *Hailstones and Halibut Bones*. New York: Trumpet Club.

Authors use colors in their stories to create moods or feelings for their readers. For example, light, bright colors, such as yellow are often used to represent warmth, happiness, or good. Dark colors can suggest coolness, sadness, or evil. Color is frequently used descriptively in *Call It Courage*. Write a color poem using one or more colors that represent concrete and abstract things from the book. Choose colors that you think represent some of the places, things, feelings, and ideas the author writes about. For example, what colors might represent the Mafatu's fear, the sea at night, the tiger shark, Uri, the octopus, Mafatu's joy when he found the whale's carcass, Mafatu's overcoming his fear, or the ridicule of his father? Remember that poetry does not have to rhyme.

Publishing an Illustrated Polynesian Dictionary

If you are not familiar with Aliki's book format, look at this book.

Aliki (1986). *How a Book Is Made*. New York: Trumpet Club.

Throughout the book, Polynesian words are used. These words are often in *italics*. The definitions of the words are imbedded in the text of the book. Keep a list of native words and their page numbers as you read. When you have finished the book, search out the meanings of the words, illustrate them, and alphabetize them. Your dictionary should have approximately twenty Polynesian terms, definitions, and illustrations. Publish your dictionary following the Aliki book format. You might want to publish in "big book" form because you will need to read your book to a group of fellow students.

Designing a Circular Time Line

Call It Courage is a "romance" novel. This means that the story has a hero, an antagonist, a big adventure, a test, events that cause the hero to become a better person, and a return to where the plot began. The story comes "full circle." Design a time line in a circular shape that encompasses the elements of a "romance" that are listed above. Especially important are the events that contributed to Mafatu overcoming his fear of the sea. Incorporate visual props such as drawings, three-dimensional objects, or even real people. Choose any format you want in designing this time line as long as the "full circle" is represented. Let your imagination be your guide.

Designing Your Own Project

If you can think of another project that will clearly demonstrate your understanding of the text, you may substitute it for one of the projects mentioned above. Talk with your teacher about this.

Belle Prater's Boy

Ruth White

The main characters in *Belle Prater's Boy*, cousins Woodrow and Gypsy, are "in that in-between place," the place Belle Prater liked so much. Woodrow's mother has disappeared, and Woodrow seems fairly calm about it. Gypsy doesn't understand this because she has never gotten over her father's death. How do young people survive without a parent? Where do they find the courage to go on?

Vocabulary	
isolated . . . . p. 3	
runts . . . . p. 4	
traipsing . . . . p. 4	
aggravate . . . . p. 9	
carcass . . . . p. 21	
pagan . . . . p. 38	
hideous . . . . p. 92	
debutante . . . . p. 126	
muddled . . . . p. 170	

"Grabbing" the Audience

The author "grabs" the reader in the first sentence of the book. The second part of the sentence, "…my Aunt Belle left her bed and vanished from the face of the earth," is particularly intriguing because she describes something that is beyond our belief. She describes this phenomenon in matter-of-fact language. Look at the openings of other novels. How does the author "grab" the reader? Try to find at least four different "grab" styles. Predict which one you think the class will like the best, and write your reasoning for this. Share these openings with the class. Ask the class to listen carefully because they will be voting on their favorite opening. Ask the class to vote. Did your prediction match their vote?

Writing an Ad

Woodrow says that he thought his mother would send him a message through the ads. Pretend that he is right and that indeed he finds a message that he believes his mother wrote to him. What does it say? Be careful of the wording. Remember where and when the story takes place. What message does Belle want to send? How will she do it so that Woodrow will be the only one to recognize and understand it?

Creating Your In-Between Place

For you, what is the place where "two worlds touch"? Where is your "in-between place"? Create a visual, either one- or three-dimensional, that shows both of the "worlds" but concentrates on your "in-between place." Be sure to show what happens in this place.

Comparing and Contrasting Characters

At first glance, Woodrow and Gypsy seem like opposites. Using a Venn diagram or other kind of visual organizer that will help you to see similarities and differences, compare and contrast the two cousins. Include specific language from the book as well as inferences and the conclusions you draw. Be sure to give the author credit when you use her exact words by enclosing them in quotation marks.

Drawing a Life Line

The character of Benny is woven throughout the story for a purpose. Create a chart or character "life line" that shows how and when Benny comes into and out of the story. Write a poem from Benny's perspective (it should be in the first person) that describes the reason for his character's being such an integral part of the story.

Making Judgments

At the end of Chapter 21, Gypsy thinks, "Sometimes impulsive is okay." Find other examples of impulsiveness in the story. Produce a visual that notes the examples of impulsiveness and the effects they caused. You might want to make a "good" list and a "bad" list. Then you would have to determine not only what is "good" and what is "bad" in the story but also who makes the judgment and for what reason.

Singing the Song

Benny sings many songs during the course of the novel. Either find recordings of these songs or someone who can sing them for you. Are there any commonalities in the melodies? In the words? Share, either by playing recordings or singing the songs, the similarities and differences in the songs.

Designing Your Own Project

If you can think of another project that will clearly demonstrate your understanding of the book, you may substitute it for one of the projects mentioned above. Talk with your teacher about this.

Dragon's Gate

Laurence Yep

Chinese men are coming to America to learn lessons they can take home with them. They learn, however, that everyone is not free and equal in America; the lessons they learn are not the same lessons that are learned by others. Otter is a young boy who struggles to get out of the great mountain's tunnel with dignity and respect. He and his friends and relatives have built a railroad they won't ever forget.

Vocabulary	
subscription	p. 2
sporadic	p. 2
nimble	p. 10
dynasty	p. 14
ingrate	p. 16
sumptuous	p. 18
tithe	p. 24
lattice	p. 28
penitently	p. 29
malicious	p. 49
envy	p. 49
debris	p. 59
cur	p. 84
rubble	p. 88
rapport	p. 115
harangue	p. 261

Understanding the Background

The book's preface describes the events that were happening in China in the 1860s. Who is the "boy emperor" that Yep talks about? Who were the Manchus, and why were they so feared? Who were the Strangers, and why were they being killed? It is necessary to understand these things to understand why many of the Chinese people were so eager to leave the familiarity of their country for an unknown land and way of life. Create some kind of graphic that will organize your information in a way that your audience can understand. What conclusions about the Chinese migration can you draw from the research you've done? Be prepared to share your conclusions with the class on presentation day.

Representing Beliefs, Customs, and Behaviors

Many of the Chinese beliefs, customs, and behaviors are very different from those in America. Choose five from the book that are foreign in nature to you. Find a visual way to represent these to the class. Tell why they are important in Chinese life. Also, choose five that are familiar to you but would probably be foreign to Chinese people. Visually represent these to the class and tell why they are important to you and your way of life.

Recognizing Differences

Uncle Foxfire was a legend to Otter when he lived in China. When Otter moves to America, he thinks differently of Uncle Foxfire. What happens in America that causes Otter to change his opinion of his uncle? Using a Chinese art form or forms (you will need to research this; begin with books by Ed Young, who was the first Chinese American to win a Caldecott Medal), create representations or symbols of Otter's "pictures" of the two sides of Uncle Foxfire. How could you capture the essence of each of the different personalities of Uncle Foxfire?

Understanding Others

As Yep describes, the Chinese people were treated inhumanely by the Americans as they worked to build the transcontinental railroad. How did they react to the poor treatment? Americans have not always treated others with kindness and understanding. Can you find another ethnic group that has been treated badly in this country? How was this group treated, and why was it treated that way? How did this group react? Perhaps you could demonstrate your findings through a play, a puppet show, a video, or some other kind of multimedia presentation. Be sure that your setting and costumes as well as your dialogue are representative of your content.

Writing from Another Perspective

Writing from a perspective other than our own is sometimes a difficult thing to do because it's difficult to let go of facts and understanding that we know (or believe) to be true. Yep describes the train from Otter's perspective on page 58, and he describes his first close look at a Westerner on page 64. Write a description of something else that Otter saw for the first time (or could have seen) either on his way to America or in America. Try to imagine what it would be like to see a familiar item for the first time. Put yourself in Otter's shoes and write the description in the first person.

Illustrating Figures of Speech

Yep uses various figures of speech throughout the novel. He uses metaphors and similes to demonstrate the comparison of the "new" or American thing to the Chinese. For example, on page 65 Yep compares a snowplow to a "monstrous arrow aimed at the heart of the mountain." On the next page, he describes the rails by saying, "The icy metal shone like the slime trails of twin snails moving relentlessly in a straight path." Create an illustrated book of figures of speech. Try to illustrate the author's exact words as accurately as you can.

Designing Your Own Project

If you can think of another project that will clearly demonstrate your understanding of the book, you may substitute it for one of the projects mentioned above. Talk with your teacher about this.

Appendix

So that you may use the titles in the first volume of this series, *Literature Circles*, we have placed each title in a conceptual grouping. Many of the titles would be appropriate in more that one concept; use your judgment.

IMAGINATION

Two Bad Ants
The Talking Eggs
The Lion, the Witch, and the Wardrobe
The Search for Delicious
The Indian in the Cupboard

DISCOVERY

Flossie and the Fox and *Mirandy and Brother Wind*
In the Year of the Boar and Jackie Robinson
Gone-Away Lake
Honey Girl
Old Yeller
The Door in the Wall
Sarah, Plain and Tall
The Westing Game
The Bone Wars

JUSTICE AND FREEDOM

The True Story of the Three Little Pigs
Number the Stars
Charley Skedaddle
Sing Down the Moon
The Sign of the Beaver
The Cay

EMPATHY

The Mitten
There's a Boy in the Girls' Bathroom
The Pinballs
The Great Gilly Hopkins
Where the Red Fern Grows

📖 COURAGE AND SURVIVAL

Lon Po Po
Trouble River
Snow Treasure
My Side of the Mountain
Julie of the Wolves
Island of the Blue Dolphins
Black Star, Bright Dawn
Hatchet
The Incredible Journey

Index

About the Authors

MIMI NEAMEN

Mimi received her BA from the University of Texas at El Paso and her MEd from the University of New Mexico; she also has an educational specialist degree from the University of New Mexico. She has published two articles, "Picture Books in the Middle School" in the *New Mexico English Journal* and "Literary Challenge: A Battle with Books" in the *New Mexico Journal of Reading*. In 1991 she and a colleague received a Quality Education Award for their development of "Literary Challenge: A Battle with Books." Mimi's interest in reading and literature and her involvement in the Rio Grande Writing Project have been the basis of many professional presentations.

In 2000, Mimi left her job in professional development to become part of a team starting a new school. The team opened the East Mountain Charter High School in August of that year. Mimi is currently the Master Teacher at the school, where she teaches and conducts professional development. She lives with her husband and five children near Tijeras, New Mexico.

MARY STRONG

Mary received her BA from the University of New Mexico and completed her MEd through the Teacher Enhancement Program, a collaborative program for midcareer teachers between the University of New Mexico and the Albuquerque Public School District. Mary and Mimi have made numerous presentations on literature circles and cooperative learning.

In 1999, Mary retired from a productive and fulfilling career in public education. She is a master gardener and spends much of her time in the garden of her mountain home in Tijeras, New Mexico, which she and her husband built after their children were grown. She is also very involved in the local charter school.

from *Libraries Unlimited*

100 MOST POPULAR SCIENTISTS FOR YOUNG ADULTS
Biographical Sketches and Professional Paths
Kendall Haven and Donna Clark

Revealing the career histories of successful 20th Century scientists, this exciting resource offers students a wonderful research tool and words of advice from great scientists on launching a science career. Much more than a collection of biographies, this is an inspiring and practical tool for students interested in science careers. **Grades 7–12.**
Profiles and Pathways Series
xv, 525p. 7x10 cloth ISBN 1-56308-674-3

BULLETIN BOARDS AND 3-D SHOWCASES THAT CAPTURE THEM WITH PIZZAZZ
Karen Hawthorne and Jane E. Gibson

This illustrated how-to guide provides detailed instructions, supply lists, and variations for an entire year (including summers and holidays) of exciting displays. Easily adapted to any subject or budget, these bulletin boards and showcases—proven favorites for students in middle and high school—will also excite the imaginations of younger students. **Grades 5–12.**
ix, 147p. 8½x11 paper ISBN 1-56308-695-6

GOTCHA!
Nonfiction Booktalks to Get Kids Excited About Reading
Kathleen A. Baxter and Marcia Agness Kochel

Booktalks and support materials for more than 350 nonfiction titles are organized according to topics popular with young readers: "Great Disasters," "Unsolved Mysteries," "Fascinating People," "Science," and "Fun Experiments To Do." These concrete, classroom-tested ideas help you effortlessly present the best of children's literature in irresistible ways. **Grades 1–8.**
xviii, 183p. 8½x11 paper ISBN 1-56308-683-2

THE INTERNET RESOURCE DIRECTORY FOR K–12 TEACHERS AND LIBRARIANS
Elizabeth B. Miller

With its curriculum-driven organization, simple instructions, and a wealth of information, this guide is simply the best Internet directory available for educators. All previous site annotations are updated as needed, and double-checked for accuracy. **All Levels.**
*Call for information on most recent edition.

STUDENT CHEATING AND PLAGIARISM IN THE INTERNET ERA
A Wake-Up Call
Ann Lathrop and Kathleen Foss

Put a stop to high-tech and more traditional low-tech forms of cheating and plagiarism. Also, learn to recognize the danger signs for cheating and how to identify material that has been copied. Sample policies for developing academic integrity, reproducible lessons for students and faculty, and lists of helpful online and print resources are included. A must-read for concerned educators, administrators, and parents. **Grades 4–12.**
xiv, 255p. 6x9 paper ISBN 1-56308-841-X

For a free catalog or to place an order, please contact:
Libraries Unlimited
Dept. B052 • P.O. Box 6633 • Englewood, CO • 80155-6633
800-237-6124 • www.lu.com • Fax: 303-220-8843